CREATING
MEMORY QUILTS

by

Madonna Auxier Ferguson

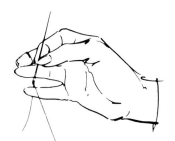

BETTY BOYINK PUBLISHING • 818 Sheldon Road • Grand Haven, Michigan 49417

Printed in U.S.A.

New Friends memory inspiration page 38
and quilt blocks 38 and 39

About the author...

Family Outing memory inspiration page 8

Madonna Auxier Ferguson is the author of several stenciling books: *XYZ of Country Stenciling, 1983* and *Stenciling, Madonna's Style Farm, Field and Wood.* Stenciling has led her from individual objects to whole scenes with each intricate part a separate stencil. Using this technique, she designed and made "First Day of School" quilt that won second prize in the National Quilting Association quilt contest in 1984.

Madonna continues her scenic stenciling in limited edition pictures she stencils in her East Lansing, Michigan home studio. Interpretating quilt blocks into scenes led to authoring a Quilter's Notebook. A series of stationery for quilters followed (Country, Four Seasons, Lakeside Views and Potpourri).

After her love of family, Madonna enjoys combining her two loves of the art/craft world by adding quilts to the interpretative shaded drawings of the country life.

In this book, Madonna takes her memories from the drawing stage through to the making of a quilt. From the antique block quilts (pages 64-73), she moves through traditional named blocks (pages 18-47), on to an exciting new dimension in contemporary quilting (pages 48-63).

Showing Off memory inspiration page 74

For
My sister, Mary Ruth, who shares
and is an important part of my memories.
My playmate and friend then . . .
my friend and soulmate now.

Flower Garden memory inspiration page 34

London Bridge

Summer Heat

Introduction

Creating a Memory Quilt

You can create a Memory Quilt without being an artist or a designer and you can make it uniquely "you." There are hundreds of traditional blocks to choose from. Just spend a quiet hour slowly reading through the index of several quilt books. Let each name roll around in your head for a few moments to see if it conjures up a memory. If so, jot it down and read on. See how many more block names you can tie in with the first. At this point, you are only interested in names, not what the block looks like. When you have a sizeable list, compare the names to the block. Some can fool you; sound so interesting, but look so plain. Others may be more complicated than you want to tackle. That's why I suggest a sizeable list. You can weed out the undesirables and still have enough for a quilt.

When you've settled on the patterns, go through the process again. This time, read the names of the blocks you've chosen and list the "colors" of your memories. Now that you have your blocks and colors, arrange the blocks in order of compatibility. This, of course, is a Sampler Memory Quilt. Samples of this type of quilt are on pages 18 and 28.

An overall Log Cabin design could be a Memory quilt too, perhaps reminiscent of your child's first tree house or your first vacation cottage. Hole in the Barn Door, representative of a summer vacation spent on a farm is one. Attic Window, a rainy day spent in Grandmother's attic could be a memory. There's no end to the possibilities. Geese on Parade quilt, sketched on page 41, is a sample of this type of memory quilt.

If you prefer to express your memories in a more contemporary manner, yet are new to contemporary design, first work it out on graph paper and then break your design down into workable sections. As with the traditional blocks, always let the "color" of your memory shine through. See contemporary section from pages 48 through 63.

Memory fabrics can also become memory quilts. Scraps from Jan's skirt, Beth's blouse, Fred's shirt would be your start. Then add memories from special occasions like a piece from a dress Mar wore to her sister's wedding. A swatch from a sunsuit will conjur up memories from a day at the beach. Cut a corner off the shirt Sar wore to his first day at school and include it in the quilt. I could g on, but I believe you can see the fun this type of memory quilt wi create. . . especially if you keep your project a secret.

Or, share the experience with a youngster or someone specia in your life by creating a quilt just with scraps from clothing wor only by that one individual. Start by rounding up as many scraps a you can right now. Then, add to your collection as special occasion occur. It may take a few years to gather enough pieces of fabric fo a full quilt or special sections in a quilt, but think of the joy th "special project" will bring as it builds toward a climax . . . a endearing memory quilt.

Keep a written record of the designs you use and the memor it represents, and as you work on your quilt, tell your story to you family and friend . This verbal recording of the quilt will be the mos interesting part. You'll "set" your family and friends to remember ing and you'll spread the joy of Creating a Memory Quilt.

Special Thanks

Special thanks to the five ladies who appliqued, pieced and quilted for me with flying fingers, sparse directions and short lead-times:

Colleen Beach, Marty Caterino, Connie Hartwick, Diana Outwin, and Patricia Humphreys.

TABLE OF CONTENTS

Topsy Turvy memory inspiration page 54

Mommy's Love memory inspiration page 8

Stella's Circle of Lilies quilt pages 55-56

Morning Song memory inspiration page 74

Visions of Sweet Things memory inspiration page 9

Practice Makes Perfect memory inspiration page 77

I'll Bake memory inspiration page 9

I'll Pick memory inspiration page 9

Family Outing

Mommy was up before the morning sun,
Getting us ready for this day's fun.
We're going to town, the oldest down to the littlest one.

We'll browse through the town to see
All the activities to be done for free.
Perhaps a puppet show for my sister and me.
Mommy and her friends will rest under a tree.
And laugh and chat while they drink their tea.

Daddy and the boys will watch the kites.
They dip and soar - a beautiful sight.
Like soft, fluffy feathers, free and light,
Only colorful, funny, fancy and bright.

We'll meet for our noonday meal and talk.
Rest, and then, continue our walk.

So many sights to see
A day of fun, and all for free,
The family together, their love the key.

Mommy's Love

On cold, dark winter nights,
Mommy sat to quilt by the coal oil light.

The stitches so fine and ever so small,
Each one perfect or not at all.

The pieces she chose from her bag of scraps,
First this one and that one so they would match.

The pink was first a dress for me,
The red a sunsuit for Sister Bea.

The blue had been Andy's pants that he wore
While learning to crawl around on the floor.

The bright yellow shirt had a hole in the arm,
Todd ripped it while out working the farm.

The brown is also on the floor in a rug
And in a Teddy for Michelle to hug.

We always knew of Mommy's deep love for us,
But she never was one to make a big fuss.

The quilt was beautiful and we were ever so proud,
It seemed to say "Mommy loves you" out loud!

See pages 45-47 for Lora's special rose quilt.

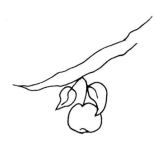

Visions of Sweet Things, If We All Help

The boys climbed the apple trees all alone,
Chose perfect apples, and carried them home.

There to be washed well and dried
Some to make jelly, others for pies.

Granny and Mommy taught us to bake and make dough,
Today, we'll bake, tomorrow, we'll sew.

Joe and Maurice carried wood for the fire
They do it for free, not for hire.

They'll wait on the porch, shuffling their feet.
Soon we'll pay them with something to eat.
Their favorite wage is pie that's sweet.

Uninvited Guests

Waves memory inspiration page 48

Daddy Counted to Ten memory inspiration page 12

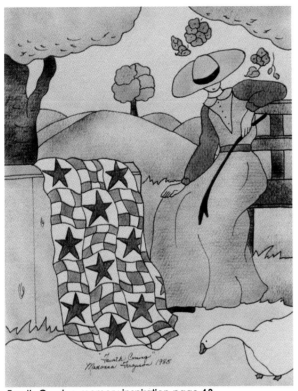

Fourth Coming memory inspiration page 13

Fourth Coming quilt pages 60-61

Barb's Lakeside Views quilt pages 49-50

Going to the Fair memory inspiration page 75

Daddy Counting to Ten

We fell in the creek, that's what we said.
We were laughing, but Daddy was mad.

Our clothes were wet clear through to our skin.
"Tell the truth!" Daddy counted to ten.

The water was warm, the day was sunny,
We tripped and fell, we thought it was funny.

Daddy said we should think some more.
He was still counting, already to four.

He counted five and then to six.
We were beginning to see we were in a fix.

We'd better think quickly before it's too late,
Two more counts and he's up to eight.

We wanted to swim, but knew it was the wrong season.
Tripping and falling seemed a good reason.

This we exclaimed as he counted to ten.
The look on his face showed how foolish we'd been.

He hugged us and loved us with a big smile,
And said we could swim, but it would be yet awhile.

He said—now Madonna and Mary Ruth,
Don't you feel better for telling the truth?

Now run inside and get out of those clothes,
You'll catch a cold, goodness knows.

We scurried inside and ran a hot tub.
Mommy had fluffy towels and gave us a rub.

We snuggled down in bed with quilts to our chins,
Still thinking aloud how much fun it had been.

Our parents were kids once, it's hard to believe.
But that must have been why we were given reprieve.

We asked Mommy and she said it was true.
All kids do it and think it is new.

How else would Daddy have known we fibbed.
We were reliving the days he had lived.

When, as a boy, into the creek he "fell."
And came up with a reason he thought would "sell."

Granddaddy Auxier had counted to ten,
He too, remembering how he'd once been.

So it goes, down through the years,
To remember it now, brings me near tears.

But they are now tears of joy,
As I count to ten for my own girl and boys.

See page 51 for a quilt made of triangles.

"Daddy Counted To Ten"
© Madonna Ferguson 1985

"Fourth Coming"
© Madonna Ferguson 1985

Fourth Coming

Today's the third of July,
My, how the year has flown by.

Seems just yesterday we picniced in the park,
our nation's independence to mark.

We took our quilt and basket of food,
Everyone there in a patriotic mood.

Tomorrow, as a family, we'll do it once more.
Chicken, potato salad, watermelon, food galore.
Many good friends and games we adore,
And, at day's end, the fireworks will soar.

See pages 60 and 61 for quilt

Grandma's House of antique block quilts pages 64-73

Goose Tracks quilt page 68

Irish Chain Variation quilt page 69

Bare Necessities memory inspiration page 16

Granny's Victory Garden quilt pages 18-19

We Can Help

Granny's Lesson memory inspiration page 76

Granny's Victory Garden memory inspiration page 17

Bare Necessities

A quilt to love, a quilt to wear,
Just as needed as a Teddy Bear.

Like the bear, it can be a good friend,
And keep you warm clear up to your chin.

They come in all colors, shapes, and sizes,
Some so pretty, they win first prizes.

Mine is simple and kind of small
You can't sleep under it if you are tall.

If you are little, you'll be just fine,
But just remember, this one is mine.

I'll show it and share it rainy or sunny,
But never could sell it, there's not enough money!

See page 69 for Irish Chain quilt variations.

Victory Garden

Our nation was still recovering from the depression when we were plunged into World War II. Furnishing our fighting men with clothing, food, and equipment became top priority, requiring personal sacrifices of America's citizens. Shortages of every kind became a way of life, and our people reacted with dignity and ingenuity, pulling together in a manner unprecedented.

As food stuffs were scarce, our people were encouraged to plant in all available spaces. Flower gardens were turned into vegetable gardens, small city yards came to life with new purpose. People who had never turned a spade of earth were digging and planting with great satisfaction. These gardens, in addition to producing food, provided an opportunity to help with the war effort. An army travels on it's stomach, hence the name, Victory Garden.

"Granny's Victory Garden"
© Madonna Ferguson 1985

"We Can Help"
© Madonna Ferguson 1985

Granny's Victory Garden

Life is hard.
　Left at home,
　　conscience of the world on my shoulders.
I said goodby to the two sons
　I carried, nursed, nurtured, guided
　　with my hands and my love.

Now both are in the hands of men.
　Did I give encouragement when needed,
　bolster ego at the proper moment.
　　Did I love loosely enough to develop
　　strength of mind, body and soul?

My heart knows I did,
　my mind won't be at ease until
　　they are safely home again.

See pages 18-27 for Granny's Victory Garden quilt and patterns.

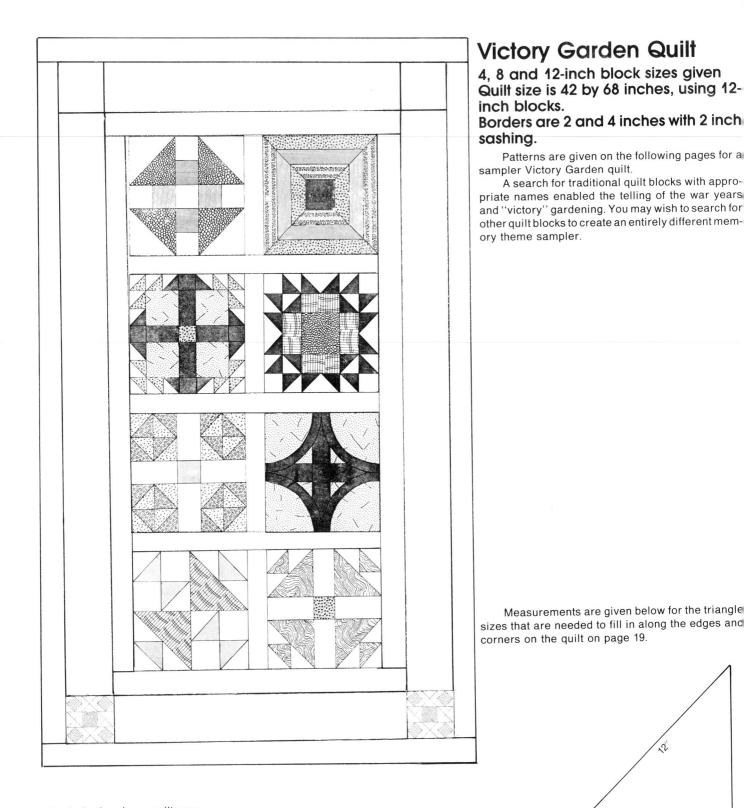

Victory Garden Quilt

**4, 8 and 12-inch block sizes given
Quilt size is 42 by 68 inches, using 12-inch blocks.
Borders are 2 and 4 inches with 2 inch sashing.**

Patterns are given on the following pages for a sampler Victory Garden quilt.

A search for traditional quilt blocks with appropriate names enabled the telling of the war years and "victory" gardening. You may wish to search for other quilt blocks to create an entirely different memory theme sampler.

Measurements are given below for the triangle sizes that are needed to fill in along the edges and corners on the quilt on page 19.

Blocks in the above quilt are:
Left row: Churn dash page 21
            Hen and chicks page 24
            Red Cross page 25
            Crosses and losses page 23
Right row: White House steps page 27
            Robbing Peter to Pay Paul page 26
            Country Cross Roads page 22
            Corn and beans page 21

            Combination Star page 20.

The Victory Garden quilt on the opposite page is a wall quilt measuring 42 by 68 inches. The above full bed size quilt uses the same victory garden patterns set on the diagonal. They are set together in rows as the vegetables of a garden are in rows.

The quilt measures 68 by 85 before adding your final border. Size adjustments can be made in the width of the border. See the opposite page for the size to make the fill in triangles along the sides and corner triangles.

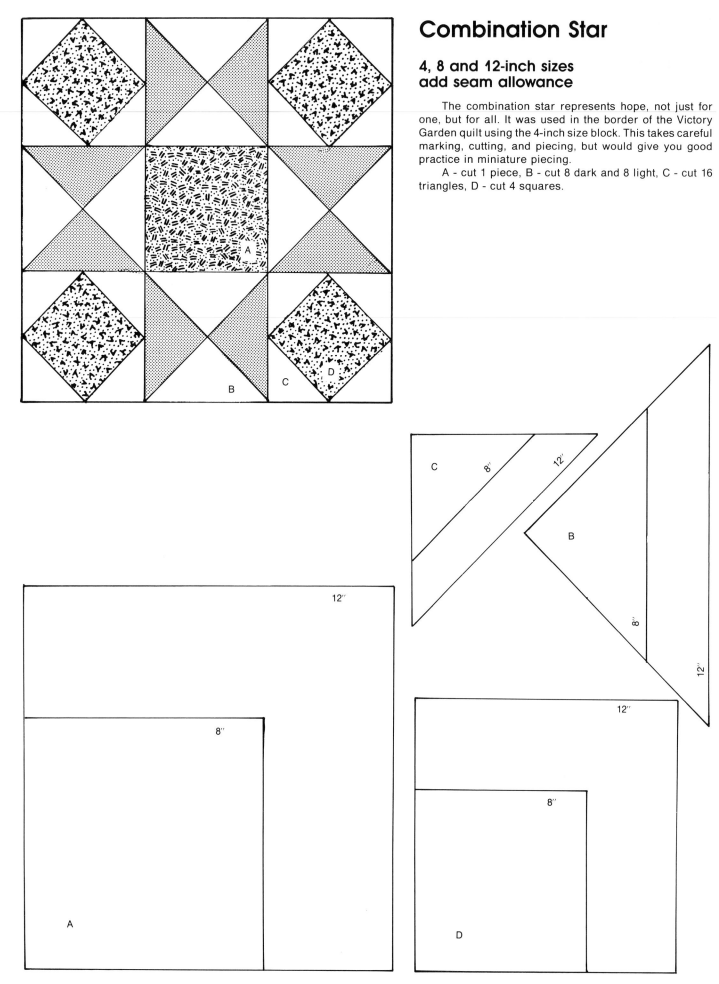

Combination Star

4, 8 and 12-inch sizes
add seam allowance

The combination star represents hope, not just for one, but for all. It was used in the border of the Victory Garden quilt using the 4-inch size block. This takes careful marking, cutting, and piecing, but would give you good practice in miniature piecing.

A - cut 1 piece, B - cut 8 dark and 8 light, C - cut 16 triangles, D - cut 4 squares.

Churn Dash

4, 8 and 12-inch sizes
add seam allowance

Every feasible way was used to economize in order to help the war effort. Churns were a part of the way of life in many homes, making butter and providing buttermilk for drinking and baking. It is no wonder that a quilter had time while churning to think of the patchwork pieces she was working on and named the resulting block "churn dash".

A - cut 4 dark and 4 light, B - cut 5 light and 4 medium.

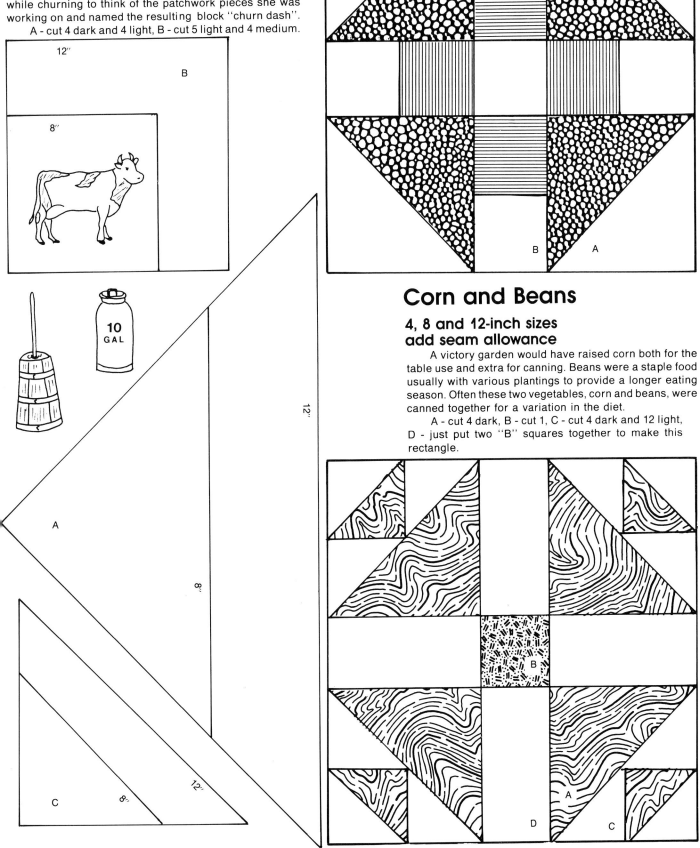

Corn and Beans

4, 8 and 12-inch sizes
add seam allowance

A victory garden would have raised corn both for the table use and extra for canning. Beans were a staple food usually with various plantings to provide a longer eating season. Often these two vegetables, corn and beans, were canned together for a variation in the diet.

A - cut 4 dark, B - cut 1, C - cut 4 dark and 12 light, D - just put two "B" squares together to make this rectangle.

Country Crossroads
4, 8 and 12-inch sizes
add seam allowance

All the peoples of our country joined together as one. A curved block requires extra care when making the templates, marking the fabric with the stitching line, careful pinning to position the two curved pieces together, stitching on the sewing line, and pressing toward the darker fabric. Clip curves to make them fit better and lay flat once stitched and pressed. Note how this looks as blocks fit together in the sketch of the quilt set on the diagonal on page 19.

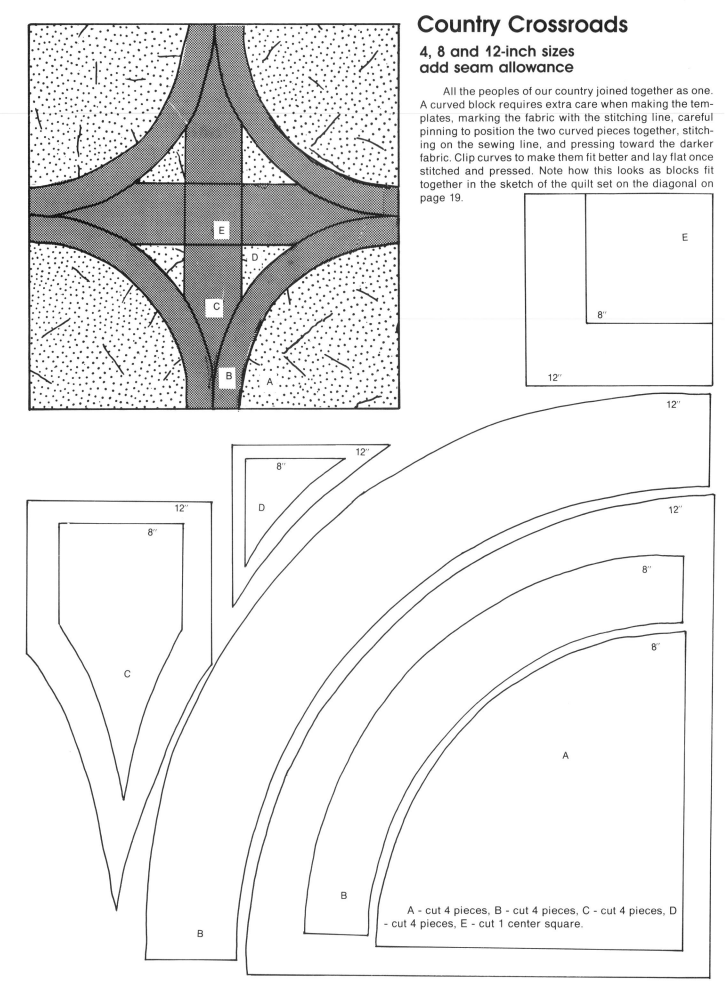

A - cut 4 pieces, B - cut 4 pieces, C - cut 4 pieces, D - cut 4 pieces, E - cut 1 center square.

Crosses and Losses

4, 8 and 12-inch sizes
add seam allowance

The name of this block says much for the faith in which a lot of families came through the losses of the times. A very simple block, some interesting designs can be achieved by the placement of the block. Make several in sketch form to twist and turn to check. Note the sketch of the row of crosses and losses on page 19.

A - cut 2 medium, B - cut 4 squares, C - cut 6 dark and 10 background.

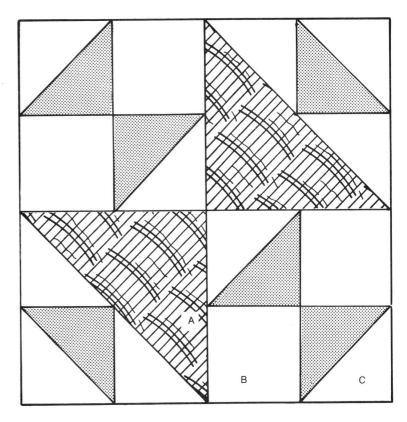

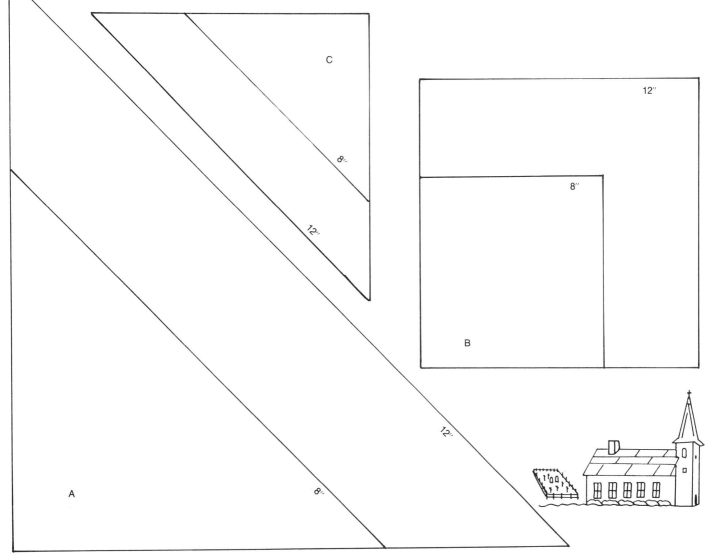

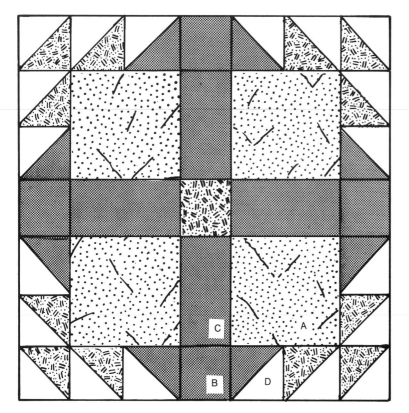

Hen and Chicks

4, 8 and 12-inch sizes
add seam allowance

Chickens were an important part of the food savings farmers enjoyed. Extra eggs could be sold for needed supplies.

This block might look a little harder, but it is just that there are more pieces than in some blocks. The contrast of small and large pieced blocks will add interest to your sampler.

A - Cut 4 light, B - cut 1 center square and 4 dark, C - cut 20 background, 8 dark and 12 medium.

Red Cross

4, 8 and 12-inch sizes
add seam allowance

The Red Cross became an important link between the servicemen and their families waiting at home.

Triangles to add interest to fill in the corners of the cross make this a good quilt to use up some of the smaller pieces left after making clothing for the family.

A - cut 4 white, B - cut 1 center square, C - cut 16 light and 16 dark triangles.

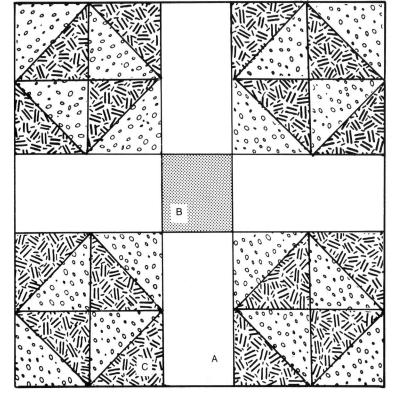

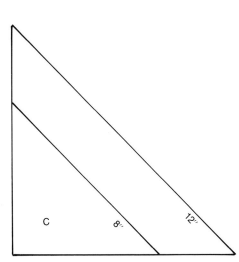

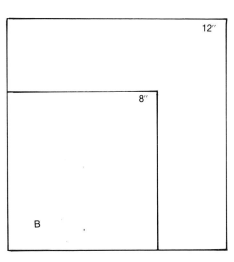

Robbing Peter to Pay Paul

4, 8 and 12-inch sizes
add seam allowance

With budgets stretched, it only takes a little imagination to bring to life the quilter using these many little pieces of left overs, thinking about making ends meet. There are many traditional quilt blocks that use this familiar name, this just being one chosen to give variety to the Victory Garden sampler quilt.

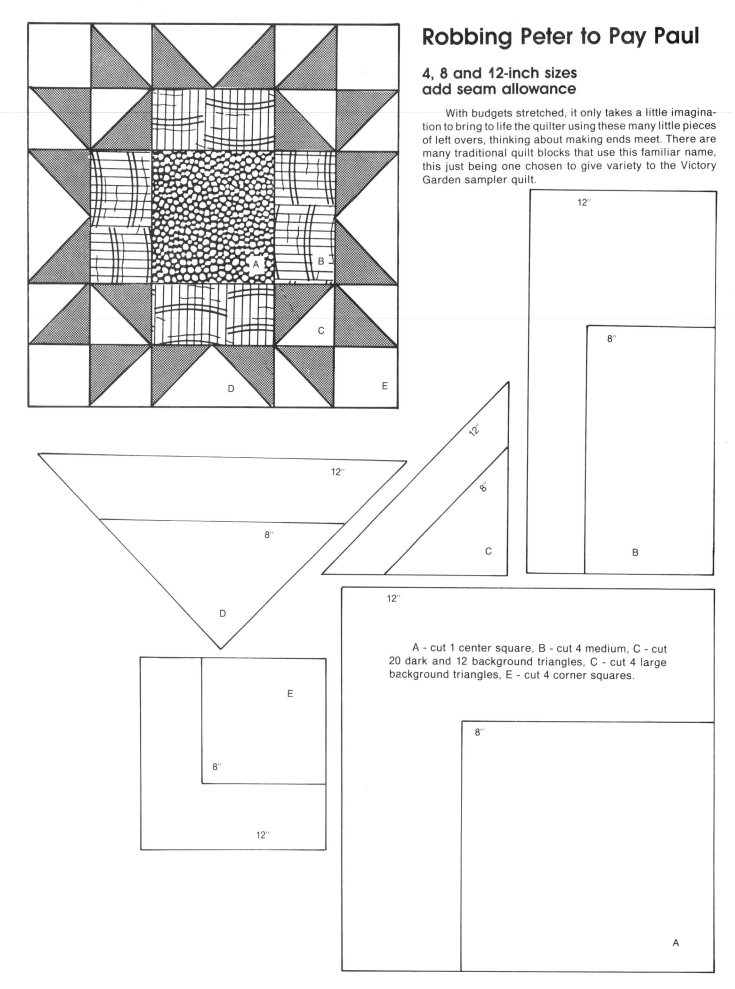

12″

8″

B

12″

8″

C

12″

8″

D

A - cut 1 center square, B - cut 4 medium, C - cut 20 dark and 12 background triangles, C - cut 4 large background triangles, E - cut 4 corner squares.

12″

E

8″

12″

8″

A

White House Steps

4, 8 and 12-inch sizes
add seam allowance

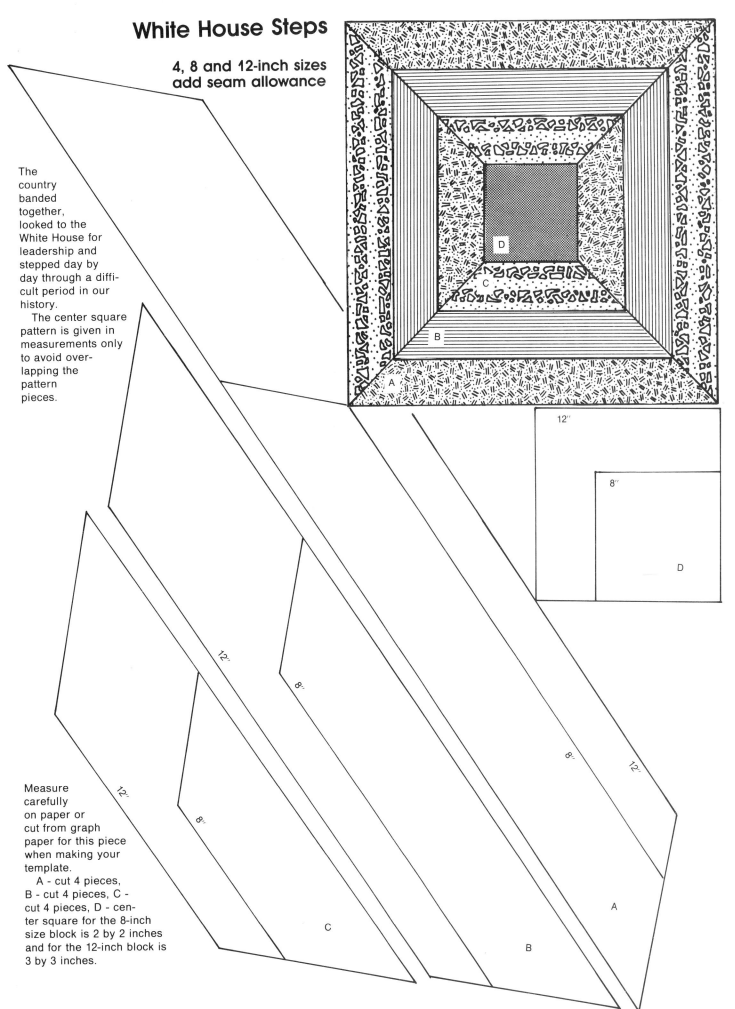

The country banded together, looked to the White House for leadership and stepped day by day through a difficult period in our history.

The center square pattern is given in measurements only to avoid overlapping the pattern pieces.

Measure carefully on paper or cut from graph paper for this piece when making your template.

A - cut 4 pieces, B - cut 4 pieces, C - cut 4 pieces, D - center square for the 8-inch size block is 2 by 2 inches and for the 12-inch block is 3 by 3 inches.

Madonna's Memory Sampler Quilt

4, 8 and 12-inch block sizes
Quilt size is 60 by 72 using 12-inch blocks
Outer borders with 9 patch corners for size adjustments.

Remember in our opening introduction about the memories that stir our thought process. We associate not only color, but thoughts that pull the past forward into the present to pick and choose ideas for making a quilt. It is some of these ideas that come to mind as I leaf through the pages of quilt books that have traditional named patterns in them.

Through this collection process, the accompanying sampler quilt is shown here in sketch form. In time, fingers will get to stitching. Then, a tangible memory piece can be passed down to my children and on to their children.

You will notice that this sampler does not have a block for Mommy. She has not been forgotten. There is a whole quilt dedicated to her, Lora's Special Rose. See pages 45-47. Also, a block is carried forward from Granny's Victory Garden series. Crosses and Losses is used to express the loss of my father, Warren, in 1975. Refer back to pattern on page 23.

The nine patch used in the outer border sections is found on page 71 in the antique block section. This would be a good, simple border to allow individual adjustments for making a quilt the size you require. The square fill in blocks are 4-inch squares. The long strips can be made by starting with a piece of paper 36 by 12-inches top and bottom (a) and 48 by 12-inches for sides (b). Mark outer center (c), connect this to inside edge (d), divide space equally by four and draw in dividing lines.

12″

8″

Greek Cross
E

Greek Cross

4, 8 and 12-inch sizes
add seam allowance

This block was chosen because the design appears to be two "F's" joined together . . . symbolizing my marriage to Gene Ferguson, the best thing that ever happened to me.

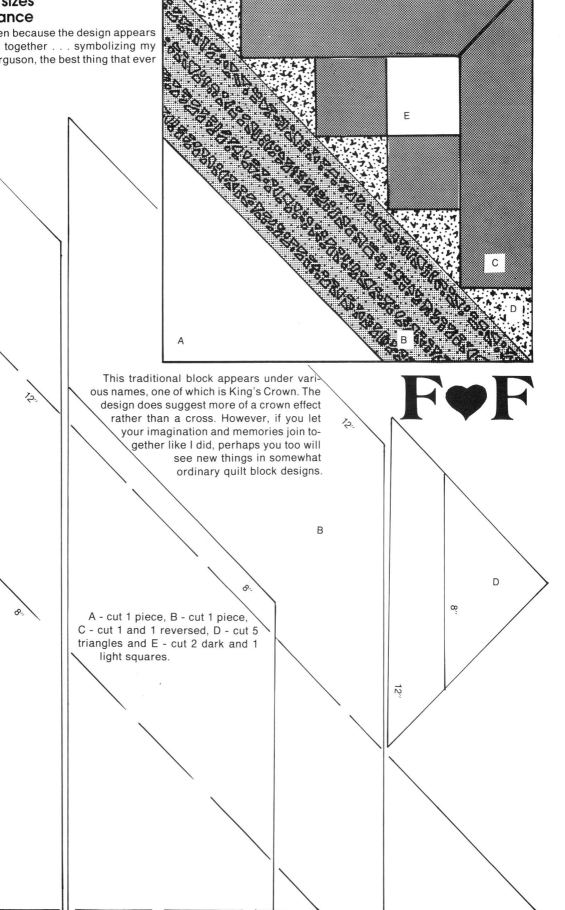

This traditional block appears under various names, one of which is King's Crown. The design does suggest more of a crown effect rather than a cross. However, if you let your imagination and memories join together like I did, perhaps you too will see new things in somewhat ordinary quilt block designs.

A - cut 1 piece, B - cut 1 piece, C - cut 1 and 1 reversed, D - cut 5 triangles and E - cut 2 dark and 1 light squares.

place on fold

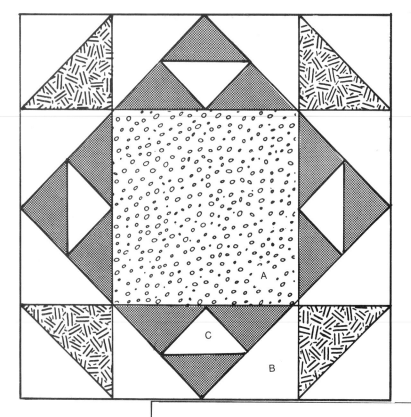

Grandmother's Favorite

4, 8 and 12-inch sizes
add seam allowance

My Granny Auxier and Granny Epperson were such important parts of my childhood, no memory quilt book would be complete without them. Every little girl feels like they are "Granny's Favorite" because of that special undisciplining, playful love a granny shares. They often have the time to sit and teach stitchery techniques that Mothers can't seem to find. See the stenciled picture and poem of "Granny's Lesson" on page 76.

A - cut 1 piece, B - cut 12 backgound and 4 medium pieces, C - cut 12 dark and 4 background pieces.

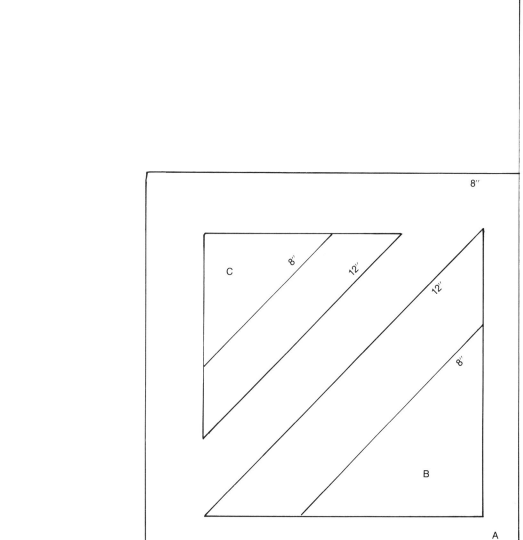

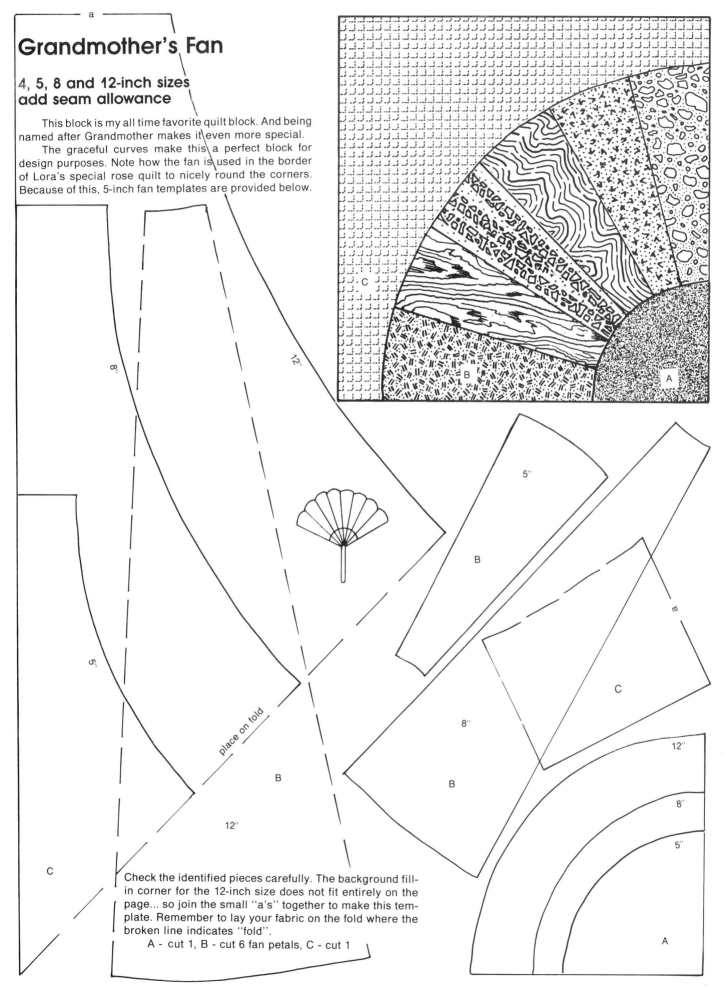

Grandmother's Fan

4, 5, 8 and 12-inch sizes
add seam allowance

This block is my all time favorite quilt block. And being named after Grandmother makes it even more special.

The graceful curves make this a perfect block for design purposes. Note how the fan is used in the border of Lora's special rose quilt to nicely round the corners. Because of this, 5-inch fan templates are provided below.

place on fold

Check the identified pieces carefully. The background fill-in corner for the 12-inch size does not fit entirely on the page... so join the small "a's" together to make this template. Remember to lay your fabric on the fold where the broken line indicates "fold".

A - cut 1, B - cut 6 fan petals, C - cut 1

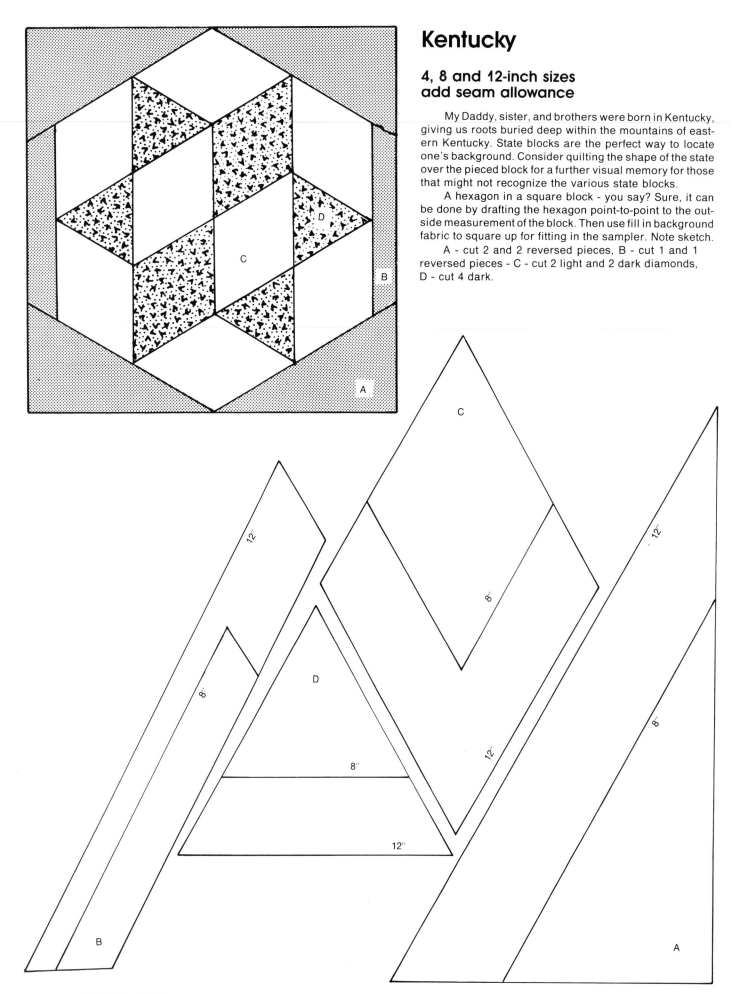

Kentucky

4, 8 and 12-inch sizes
add seam allowance

My Daddy, sister, and brothers were born in Kentucky, giving us roots buried deep within the mountains of eastern Kentucky. State blocks are the perfect way to locate one's background. Consider quilting the shape of the state over the pieced block for a further visual memory for those that might not recognize the various state blocks.

A hexagon in a square block - you say? Sure, it can be done by drafting the hexagon point-to-point to the outside measurement of the block. Then use fill in background fabric to square up for fitting in the sampler. Note sketch.

A - cut 2 and 2 reversed pieces, B - cut 1 and 1 reversed pieces - C - cut 2 light and 2 dark diamonds, D - cut 4 dark.

California

4, 8 and 12-inch sizes
add seam allowance

My brother Joe and his wife, Shirley, moved to California twenty-five years ago. With their five children and eleven grandchildren, they have established quite a clan of Auxiers on the west coast.

This block does not provide long seams straight across for easy piecing. However, if you tip the block on point, you can see a nine-patch effect that provides easier piecing with longer seams once the three units are pieced.

A - cut 4 background, B - cut 4 pieces, C - cut 4 medium and 1 dark.

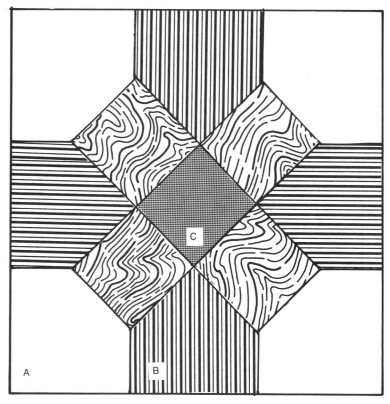

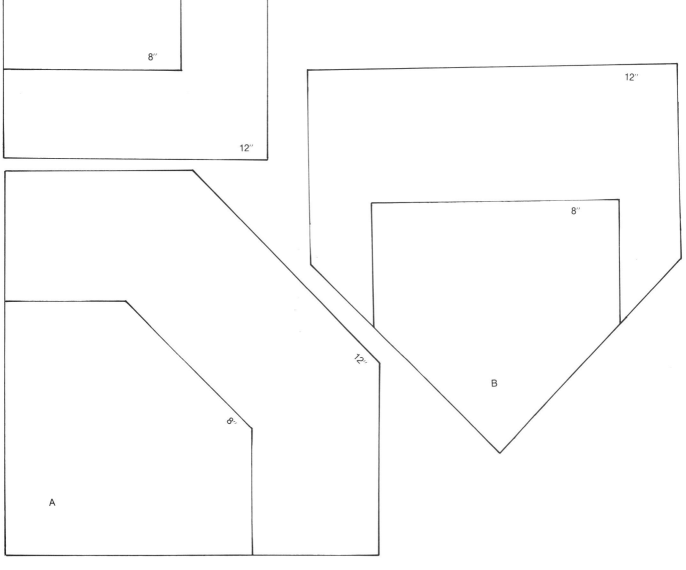

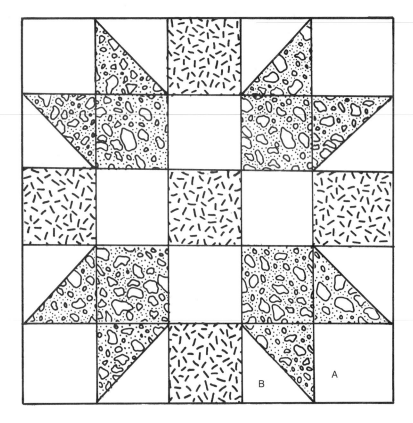

Sister's Choice

4, 8 and 12-inch sizes
add seam allowance

I couldn't have chosen a better block for naming after my sister, Mary Ruth. With two brothers and one sister, you can understand why she is the "choice". There is a bond of playing, sharing and caring between sisters that can be a life-long memory. See page 3 for some of these memories.

Sister's Choice is an equally divided block that pieces nicely in rows.

A - cut 8 light, 5 medium, and 4 dark; B - cut 8 dark and 8 light.

Flower Garden

Pretty red geraniums all in a row,
First we plant, then we hoe,
"Why?" you ask - 'cause Granny told us so'.

We may be little, but we're not dumb,
We listen to Granny with her green thumb,
We worked very hard and are almost done,
Granny, are you sure this is supposed to be fun?

We'll have to water then we'll weed,
Yes, we know, it'll be a good deed,
We'd rather do this than give the chickens the feed.

"Yes," Granny said, "they'll get plenty of sun,
But she answered all our questions but one
Is this really supposed to be fun?

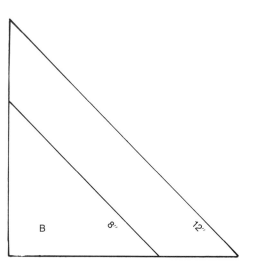

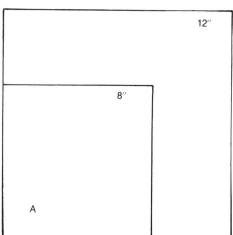

"Flower Garden"
© Madonna Ferguson 1985

King's Crown

4, 8 and 12-inch sizes
add seam allowance

My brothers are seven and nine years older than me. Older brothers, when you are all at home and still growing, have a way of getting you to do their bidding. It is as if they were kings and I was their subject. We all grow up and look back on those memories with laughter.

With the right choice of fabrics, one can achieve a crown effect with the larger, dark triangles and the jewels around the crown in the medium smaller triangles.

A - cut 1 piece, B - cut 4 background squares, C - cut 4 dark triangles, D - cut 8 medium triagles.

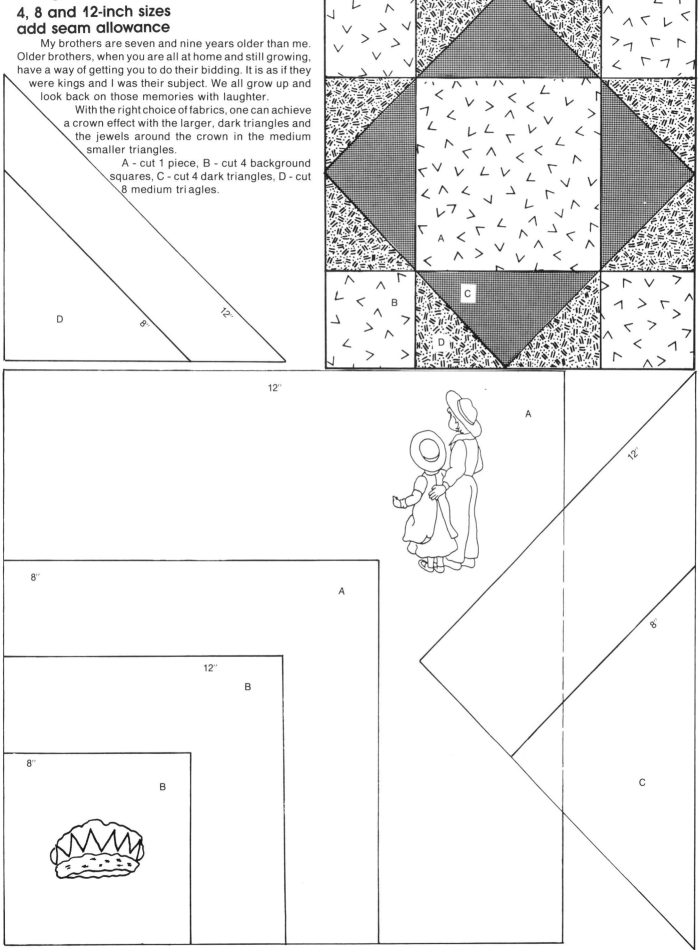

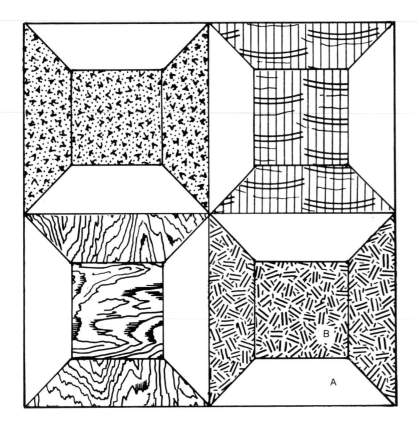

Spools

4, 8 and 12-inch sizes
add seam allowance

A spool is representative of my entry into the wonderful world of quilting. Thread is the glue to bonding fabric pieces together much as love is the glue to bonding families together. A love of quilting seems to expand one's memories to overflowing many times because of the "family" of quilters.

What a simple little block that offers so very many design possibilities. Try this one for a whole scrap quilt keeping each spool square and ends of the same fabric. Or, this might be the perfect block for your sampler of memories quilt. Since it takes four individual spools to achieve the twisting effect, four are included for the block as the sketch indicates.

A - cut 8 background and 8 dark pieces, B - cut 4 squares.

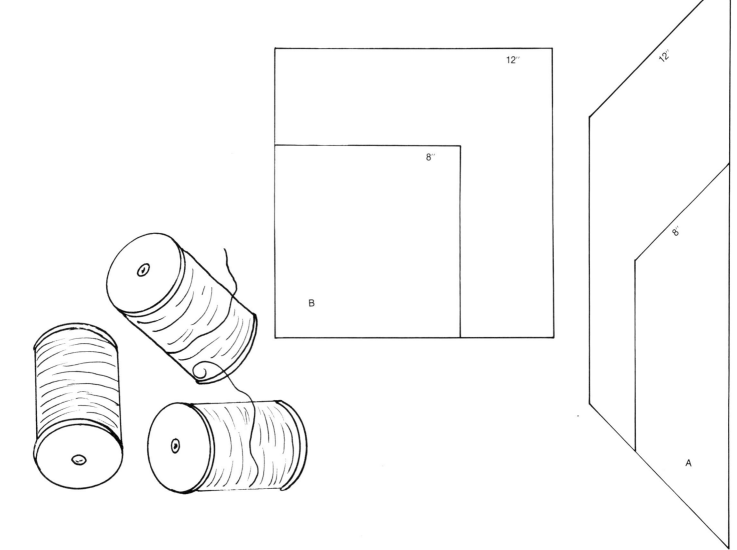

Peony

4, 8 and 12-inch sizes
add seam allowance

Huge clumps of pink and white peonies always adorned our front yard on the farm. Flowers can be an important part of our growing up, therefore we often have fond memories of flowers. From the flowers we pick to take to Mommy as a youngster (often her prize showpiece) to the dance corsages of a beau, a wedding bouquet, to the flowers of a loving husband.

Sometimes this traditional block is referred to as a leaf. Your choice of fabrics would seem to make it look like a cluster of flowers. The whole stem square is given. This stem may be appliqed onto a solid square, or it may be pieced using the pattern below.

A - cut 4, B - cut 4 background, 1 center, 12 in flower colors, C - cut 16 flower and 16 background triangles, D - cut 4 stem units.

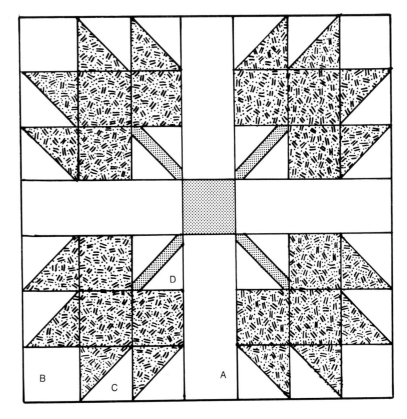

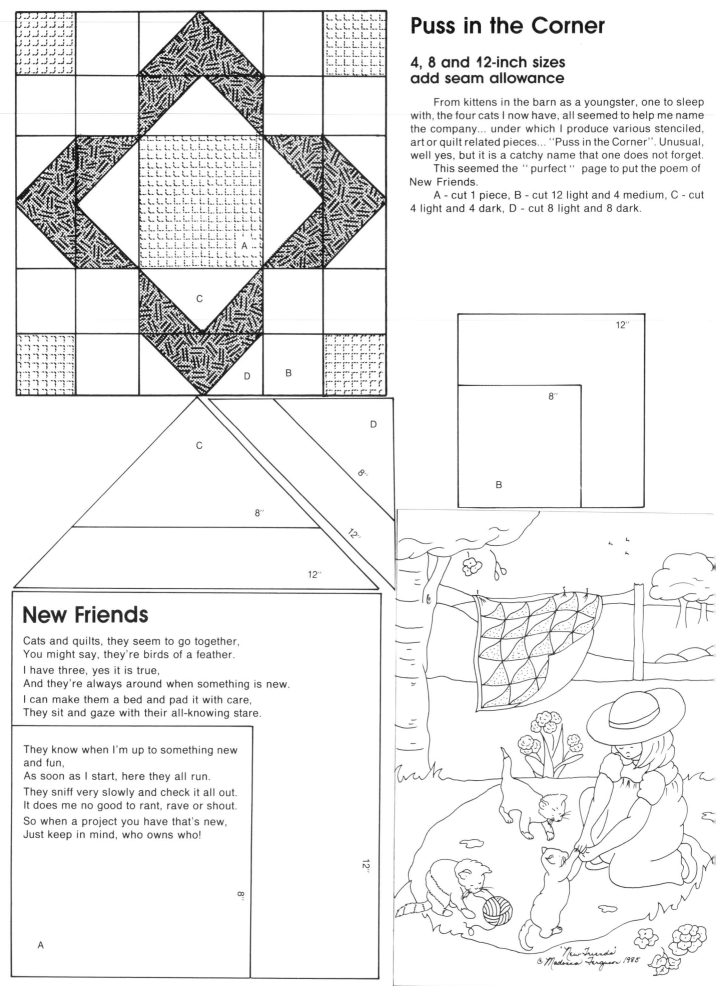

Puss in the Corner

4, 8 and 12-inch sizes
add seam allowance

From kittens in the barn as a youngster, one to sleep with, the four cats I now have, all seemed to help me name the company... under which I produce various stenciled, art or quilt related pieces... "Puss in the Corner". Unusual, well yes, but it is a catchy name that one does not forget.

This seemed the "purfect" page to put the poem of New Friends.

A - cut 1 piece, B - cut 12 light and 4 medium, C - cut 4 light and 4 dark, D - cut 8 light and 8 dark.

New Friends

Cats and quilts, they seem to go together,
You might say, they're birds of a feather.

I have three, yes it is true,
And they're always around when something is new.

I can make them a bed and pad it with care,
They sit and gaze with their all-knowing stare.

They know when I'm up to something new and fun,
As soon as I start, here they all run.

They sniff very slowly and check it all out.
It does me no good to rant, rave or shout.

So when a project you have that's new,
Just keep in mind, who owns who!

Cats and Mice

4, 8 and 12-inch sizes
add seam allowance

We grew up on a farm, you know!

This traditional block is used here in this sampler quilt as one of the memory blocks. Memories are fun. So, look at the fun you can have with the corner to corner direction of the dark fabrics in the Tic Tac Toe quilt on page 58. It does give direction when used in this way - what a perfect "X" block.

A - cut 4 background, B - cut 12 light and 8 dark, C - cut 5 squares.

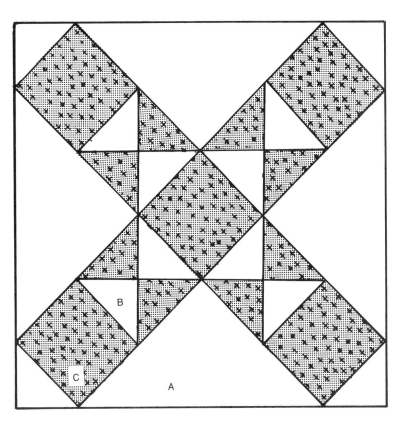

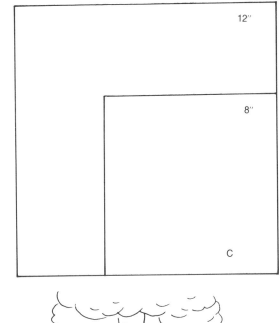

Geese on Parade

4, 8 and 12-inch size blocks
Quilt size is 46-inch square using 8-inch blocks, 69-inch square using 12-inch blocks.
Flying geese border i 4-inches for 8-inch blocks, 6-inches fo 12-inch.
Sashing is 2-inches fo 4-inch blocks, 3-inches for 12-inch blocks.

Imagination is an impor tant factor in quilt block nam ing. Our ancestors had grea imaginations. The airiness o two triangles, one light and on dark, have often led quilters t name blocks of this type afte geese.

Artists depicting the country scene often use geese for ground area fill-in to add interest. As a country artist and as a quilter, this geese quilt pulled the two together for an effective wall quilt. This wall hanging would feel right at home in any country decor theme. You may enjoy using the playful geese throughout the pattern pages as quilting ideas.

Geese flock together, quilters do too! The Hands All Around block holding the corner position in the borders was used to express the feelings I have whenever I'm around quilters. Everyone sharing, supporting, like a fam- ily joins hands before sharing a meal, friends joining hands while singing, or perhaps strangers joining hands in Church before prayer.

Top row blocks are Dutchman's Puzzle page 41 and Goose Tracks page 42. Bottom row blocks are Flying Geese page 44 and Geese to the Moon page 42. Flying Geese border page 41 and corner block Hands All Around page 43.

Dutchman's Puzzle,
Flying Geese Border

4, 8 and 12-inch sizes
add seam allowance

Two templates are all that are required to give a flying geese effect, center one a larger dark fabric with the two fill-in triangles a lighter background fabric. The same templates are used for the block and the flying geese bordering the four blocks.

A – cut 8 (4 center ones may be darker with 4 outer ones medium), B – cut 16 fill-in triangles.

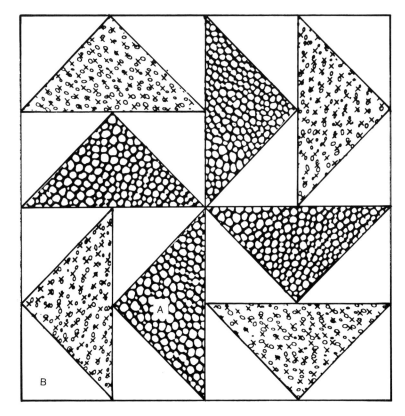

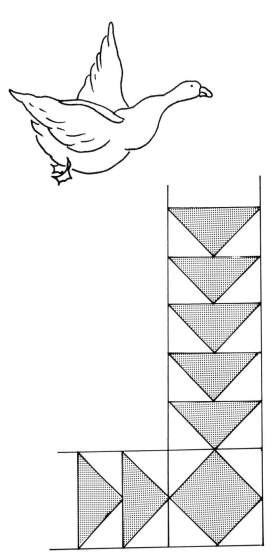

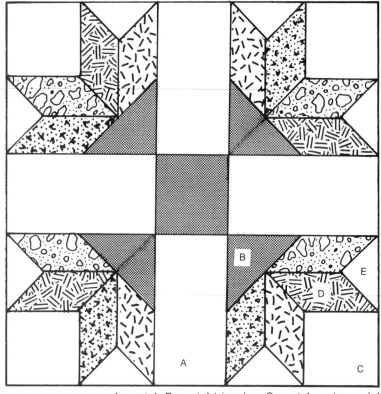

A – cut 4, B – cut 4 triangles, C – cut 1 center and 4 background squares (pattern on next page), D – cut 8 and 8 reversed, E – cut 8 triangles.

Geese to the Moon

4, 8 and 12-inch sizes
add seam allowance

A – cut 4, B – cut 16 dark and 16 light triangles, C – cut 1 center square (pattern on next page).

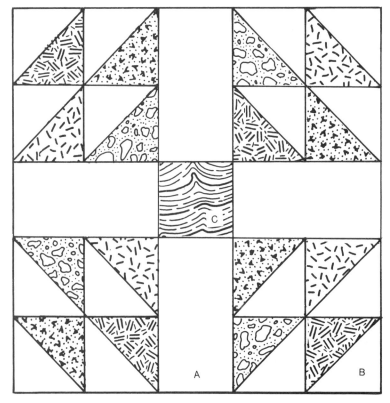

Goose Tracks

4, 8 and 12-inch sizes
add seam allowance

With many of the same templates required for the three blocks on these two pages, the patterns are facing pages. This will save you time when making the Geese on Parade quilt on page 40. See antique quilt sketch on page 68.

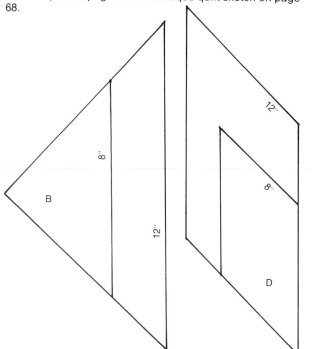

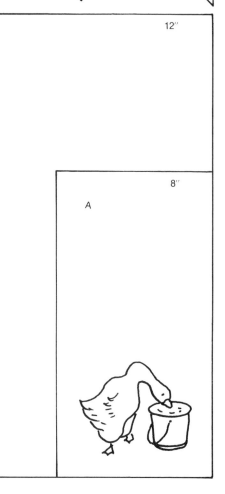

Hands All Around

4, 8 and 12-inch sizes
add seam allowance

Although this is not the easiest of blocks to piece because of the curved piecing, it is well worth the effort. Extra care also needs to be taken when cutting the pattern piece D out as well because of having to cut eight with the template in one direction, then turning it upside down to give the reversed eight required. This "D" pattern piece is on page 42. Piece the four D pieces together first, add the corner square and fill-in triangles. Add four B pieces to the curved edges of A. Then you are ready to put the block together.

A – cut 1, B – cut 4, C – cut 8, D – cut 8 and 8 reversed (Pattern is on preceding page), E – cut 8 fill-in triangles.

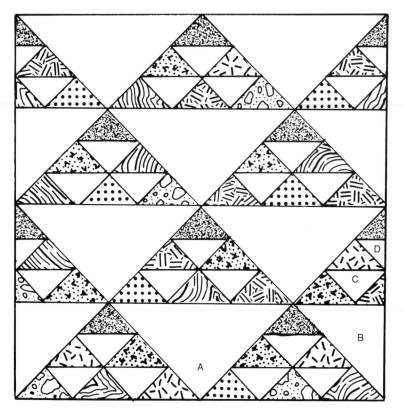

Flying Geese

4, 8 and 12-inch sizes
add seam allowance

The flying geese pattern makes an excellent scrap quilt block to use for an overall quilt. Here we have used one single block for the Geese on Parade sampler.

You will notice that a predominate darker shade was used for the top triangle of each grouping. This helps give the feeling of the "V" one sees as the Canadian geese fly overhead in this formation.

A - cut 6 pieces, B - cut 4 pieces, C - cut 44 dark and 22 light, D - cut 8 dark and 4 light.

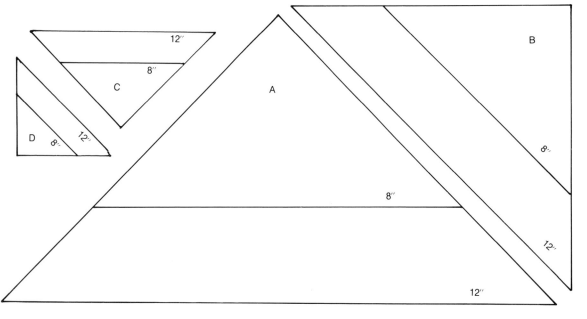

Lora's Special Rose

Somewhere there is a special four
   petaled rose,
Each petal developes as each of my
   children grows.
It's joined with Mommy's and Daddy's
   hands all around,
In the center, four hearts are to be
   found.
Half roses join the hands as if to view
My four beautiful children as they grew.

While they grew, some tall, some shorter,
My love applied, like bricks, with mortar.
Memory quilt follows on pages 46–47.

Lora's Special Rose Quilt

Lora's Special Rose Quilt
20-inch applique blocks
Quilt size is 96 by 108 inches.
Width of inner border pieces are 2, 4 and 6-inches.
Outer border is 6 inches.
Headboard quilt size 32 by 52 inches.
Inner border around blocks is 1 inch.
Outer border with fan corners is 5 inches.

Headboard quilt on inside back cover.

I've told my mother how much I love her, I've expressed that love on her birthday, Mother's Day and Christmas with carefully chosen gifts, some I've made with my own hands with thoughts of love. But as I grew older, and she grew older, I felt the need, once more, to honor her and her love.

Mommy, this quilt design and poem are for you. I truly do appreciate all you've done for me and for your love which continues to flow.

This makes a lovely appliqued quilt. A rectangle bed size quilt is easily achieved by allowing the inner borders around the blocks to go to the side edges. But when it comes time to add the top and bottom borders, they go to the outside edge of the inner borders. Note sketch.

You may choose to just square off (see illustration "a") or to miter (see illustration "b") when adding the three inner borders around the blocks. For an interesting variation, note how the sketch is done.

The Headboard quilt was appliqued and quilted by Patricia Humphreys, Charleston, West Virginia.

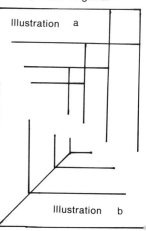

Illustration a

Illustration b

Lora's Special Rose Block

**20-inch applique block
add seam allowance**

Center the design on a 20-inch background block
(plus seam allowance).

add seam allowance

Waves

Mom took us to the beach to play in the sun,
Swim, picnic, and share in the fun.

I'll build a castle as tall as me,
Mommy will read and rest by the sea.

She'll stretch out on her lovely old quilt,
And admire the beautiful castle I've built.

Joe will play ball, he's older than me,
He'll play in the waves, clear up to his knees.

He coaxes and teases me to be brave
Not me, I'm afraid of the waves.

Mommy said not to worry I'm small,
For one of these days, I'll be brave and tall.

Let's eat our lunch and take a rest,
This day at the beach, one of the best.

Barb's Lakeside Views

8-inch Roman Stripe block
2-inch pieced borders
Quilt size is 42 inches square.

My friend and co-worker, Barb Dundore, along with her husband, Dick are spending their first summer in their new (to them) lakeside condominum. This version of the Roman Stripe is to celebrate their new home and the view from their deck of graceful sailboats. Shades of grayed blues and greens were used for the water and mauve, golds and soft yellows for the sky. The off-white triangles represent sailboats.

The use of the roman stripe pattern and dull colors are reminiscent of old Amish quilts. Border patterns and the basic 8-inch triangle pattern to cut the sewn strips from are on this page and page 50. More details on working with the Roman Stripe block are on page 53.

A – 16 dark, 16 light Roman stripe triangles, B – 4 and 4 reversed C – 12 light, D – 8 darkest, E – 4 dark and 4 light, F – 6 and 6 reversed G – 12 light.

Barb's Lakeside View quilt was pieced and quilted by Connie Hartwick of Mason, Michigan.

Barb's Lakeside Views quilt on page 11.

dark and 1

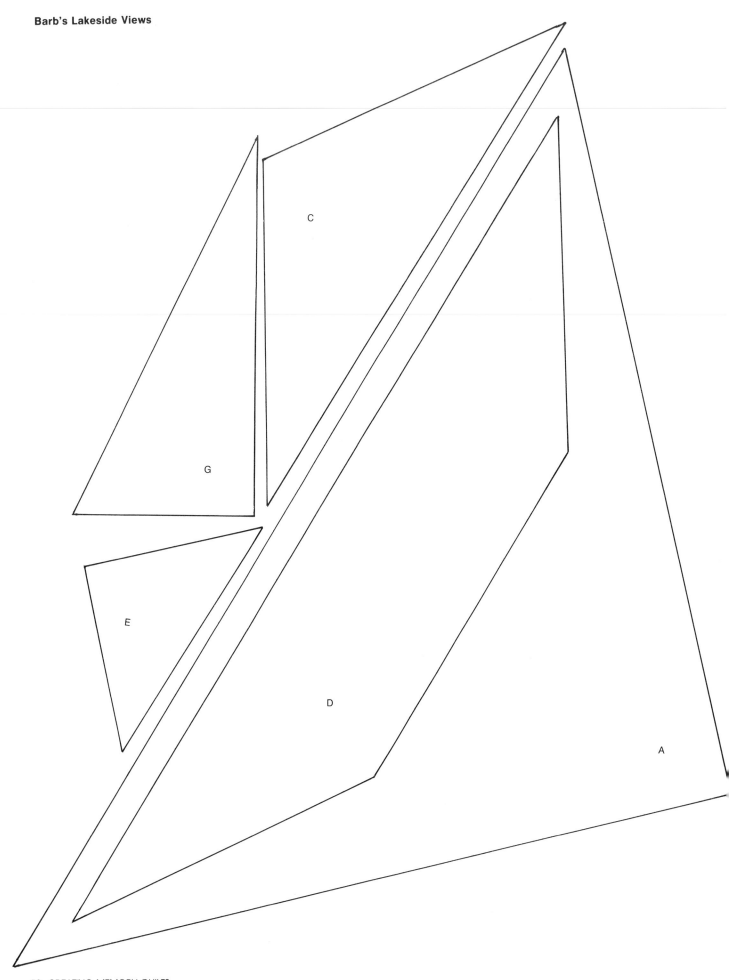

Trapped

3-inch Triangle
Quilt size is 25 by 35 inches
Border size is 5 inches.

The heritage of quilting needs to be passed down to our children. How else will the art/craft form be preserved that has provided so rich a history to so many. Begin with a simple shape.

Last summer, our daughter, Michelle, cut many three-inch triangles of nine different colors and had great fun laying out a small wall hanging. She was fascinated by how moving just two triangles could change the whole feeling of the piece.

Perhaps this could be a joint project with your son or daughter with them choosing the colors and color placement. This, too, could be a "Memory Quilt." The time spent choosing colors and the small talk that automatically occurs will evoke fond memories in their later years. You will already have "stitched" one memory into the quilt. You could remind them of their favorite dress, shirt or baby quilt so that color could be used. Encourage them to express some of their memories in colors. You will be pleasantly surprised as they get into the swing of it. They will bring up experiences you have forgotten. What fun to spend an afternoon turning back the clock with the fond memories ticking away.

A solid black border was chosen to frame the triangle design. But then a binding fabric of two of the colors was strip pieced to add color in the binding. See this quilt in color on the back cover.

By varying the size of triangle, you could make the quilt shown in "Daddy Counted to Ten" scene on page 10, or the doll quilt shown in "Lora's Special Rose" scene on the inside back cover.

This quilt designed and pieced by Michelle Ferguson, East Lansing, Michigan. Quilted by "Mom."

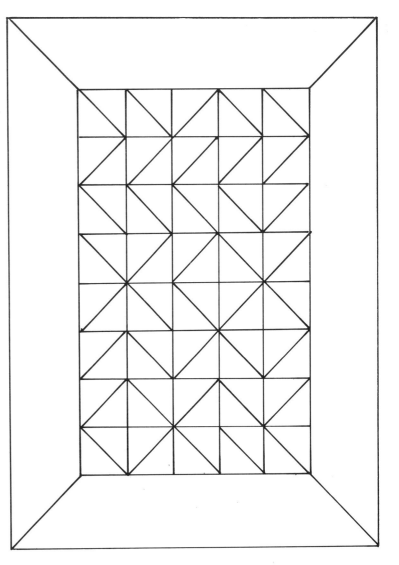

Homework

Ah, Mom, I'm hungry, I need a snack,
It's late and time to hit the sack.

My stomach hurts, it really does,
My eyes are watering, full of fuzz.

The cats are meowing and I can't think,
Andy broke my pencil, the little fink!

Five more pages before I'm through,
I'm not sure when they're due.

Maybe they can wait awhile,
Mom, are you beginning to smile?

Does that mean I can take a break?
Oh, Mom, for pity sake!

See color photograph of Trapped over Michelle's desk on the back cover.

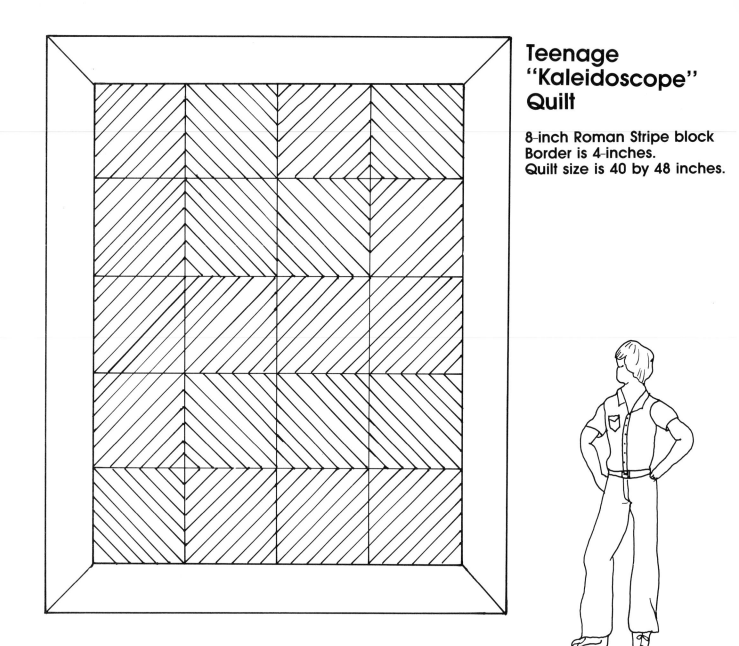

Teenage "Kaleidoscope" Quilt

8-inch Roman Stripe block
Border is 4-inches.
Quilt size is 40 by 48 inches.

Teenagers are searching for their own identities, aching to strike out on their own, forming individual personalities and opinions, developing values, setting goals. Part child, part adult, they can change from one to the other and back again within just a few moments, just as a kaleidoscope changes as you turn it. After seeing my first son through his teens, I told my other two children they had to skip those years and go from twelve to twenty. However life doesn't work that way, and I now have two more teenagers. I am enjoying them and wouldn't have it any other way. As usual, the second and third children do not have to be perfect. Maybe that comes with mothers growing a little older with the knowledge that no one is perfect, even one's self.

This version of the Roman Stripe was designed with teenagers in mind; lots of different colors with varying shades of the same colors to reflect their different moods and characteristics. Lots of brights, especially yellows to reflect the morning sun. (Teenagers are in the "morning" of their lives and we mothers need all of the sunshine we can get!) I usually work with muted colors, but points were scored with my son, Andy with the brightness of this quilt. It's the first quilt I designed that he asked to be hung in his room.

Shading of the quilt was left open for you to color in your ideas. Teenage Kaleidoscope quilt was pieced and quilted by Colleen Beach of Lansing, Michigan.

"Kaleidoscope" quilt on back cover.

Roman Stripe

4-inch illustration & 8-inch pattern add seam allowance

The 8-inch pattern for your use in making the template is found on page 50 where it was used for Barb's Lakeside View quilt.

Fabric requirements for the Teenage Kaleidoscope quilt: 1/2 yard of 12 different fabrics, 1-1/2 yard for borders and binding, 1-1/2 yard backing and batting.

Cut fabric 7/8-inch wide by 45 inches long. Sew eight colors together using the standard quilter's 1/4-inch seam allowance. (See illustration A). When sewing, start at opposite ends to help keep the fabric from twisting. From each set of eight, you will be able to get 5 triangles. (See illustration C).

Kaliedoscope requires 40 triangles. A good assortment to begin arranging would be to make 3 strips or 15 triangles from one set of colors, 2 strips or 10 triangles, 2 strips of different color arrangement or 10 more triangles and a final color set of 8 sewn strips to cut 5 more triangles to make the 40 required.

When making the sets use some of the same colors. When sewing, change the order of placement and they will be different.

Press seam allowances all in one direction. Cut out triangles with template, then play with order in which is pleasing to you. Sew the triangles into squares, squares into rows, and the rows into your kaliedoscope quilt.

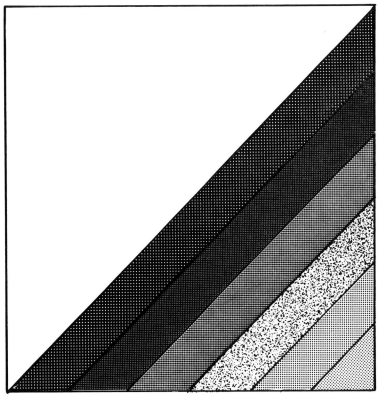

Illustration A - Join strips of fabric

Illustration B - Press seams in one direction toward darker fabrics.

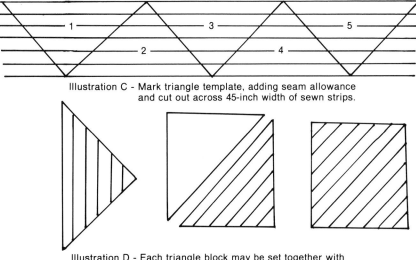

Illustration C - Mark triangle template, adding seam allowance and cut out across 45-inch width of sewn strips.

Illustration D - Each triangle block may be set together with solid triangle or with another pieced triangle.

Topsy Turvy II

Look, Mary Ruth, see what I can do.
Who's upside down, me or you?

You're on Granny's lily quilt I see.
Who's in trouble, you or me?

She chose the colors especially for Granddad.
Get it dirty and she'll be mad.

It's their colors; a lily fantasy,
For their bed, not for under a tree.

She gave her permission you say?
Then, move over, I'm on my way.

Stella's Circle of Lilies Quilt

20-inch quilt block
Add seam allowance

This pattern was drawn a few years ago when my Granny, Stella Epperson, was ill as a tribute to her love. The circular design represents the many times I've felt safe and warm within the circle of her protective arms.

Granny got well, I got busy, the design was laid aside, and for awhile, forgotten. But, when the planning of this book began, the design leaped to my mind once more. Granny is ninety-five this year and I'm proud to share her circle of love with you.

Both large and small prints were used giving added dimension to the design. The tulips were cut from a large flame stitch, the leaves were cut from a large floral chintz, and the remaining pieces from small prints. The stems were cut from the reverse side of a small print.

The quilt block sample shown in color on page 6 was appliqued and quilted by Marty Caterino, East Lansing, Michigan.

add seam allowance

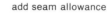

Stella's Circle of Lilies Quilt

20-inch quilt block
Quilt size is 80 x 100-inches
Border is 10-inches

Twelve twenty inch quilt blocks are required for making a full size quilt of the lily pattern. Add a ten-inch border to give a good amount of room for some extra quilting and you have the perfect size quilt. A section of one of the circles from tulip through tulip is appliqued in the corners (a ten-inch square).

Three Special Memories

"You don't write about us," Andy said.
"Only about your brothers, sister, Mommy and Dad."

"But, Andy," I allowed,
"You weren't around when I was a child.

These are my memories I'm sharing you see."
But," He said, "What about Todd, Michelle and me?

When you are eighty and looking back, I'll bet,
You'll find we were memories that hadn't happened yet.

You are now writing about times and people we don't know.
All the while, we're memories continuing to grow.

We can't rhyme and we can't draw,
Who's to put down the things we saw?"

"Andy," I said, "your time will come,
When you'll tell your kids of all your fun.

But, for now, so you won't feel left out,
Stomp your feet, and in frustration, shout.

Here you all are,
My very best memories by far."

See the back cover for these three memories and the Teenage "Kaleidoscope" quilt inspired by this conversation with Andy is on page 54-55.

"Three Special Memories"
© Madonna Ferguson 1985

Madonna's "Tic Tac Toe" Wall Quilt

4, 8 and 12-inch sizes
Quilt size with 4-inch - 18 inches
Quilt size with 8-inch - 38 inches
Quilt size with 12-inch - 47 inches

The existing Tic Tac Toe traditional quilt blocks shown reviewed were not found very interesting. The two blocks shown here, Queen's Crown and Cats and Mice, are ideal for a wall hanging for a game room, family room, office, or child's room. Let your choice of colors depend on where you wish to hang your finished quilt.

To make a playable wall hanging, piece nine solid blocks 1-inch larger than the size block using, i.e. 4-inch would require 5-inch solid block. Add borders and quilt this solid quilt. Make your "X" and "O" blocks the size needed into bound off squares with Velcro attached to the back. This would make a great gift for a man or young boy. Here's an opportunity to create a playful memory when creating a quilt.

The cats and mice pattern and templates are found on page 30 as one of the blocks in Madonna's memory sampler. Templates A and B were used in the border corners.

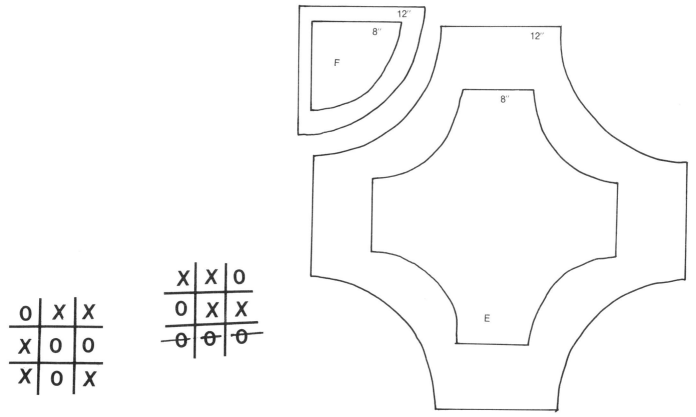

Queen's Crown

4, 8 and 12-inch sizes
add seam allowance

Traditional quilt blocks offer few truly round designs. In designing our block heritage, our ancestors shied away from the round shapes to avoid difficult piecing. But for making a tic tac toe quilted fun piece, a round design had to be found. What a beautiful quilt block design this is standing alone or used as it is here. Careful marking, cutting and piecing will make this an easier block than you might think.

A - cut 4, B - cut 4, C - cut 4, D - cut 4, E - cut 1, F - cut 4.

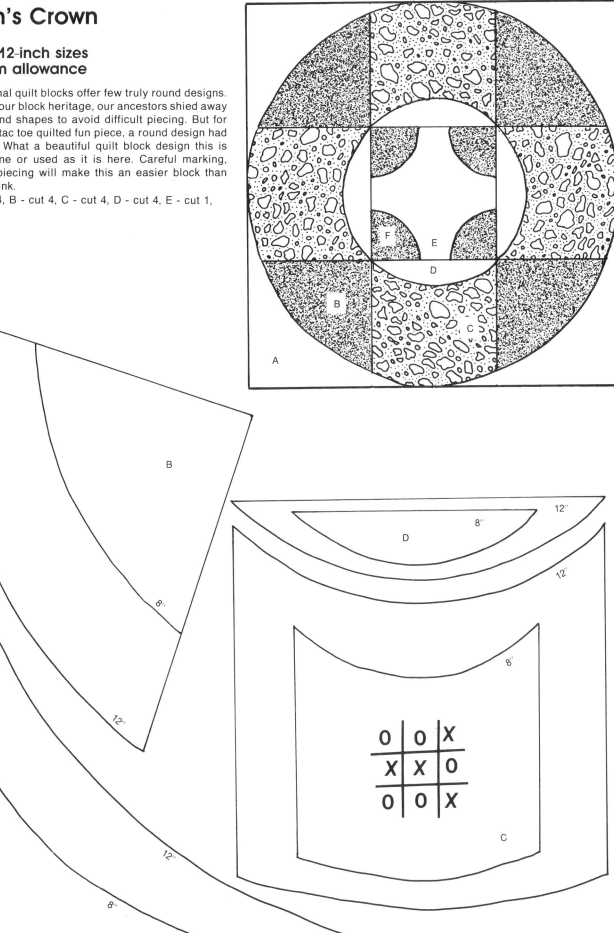

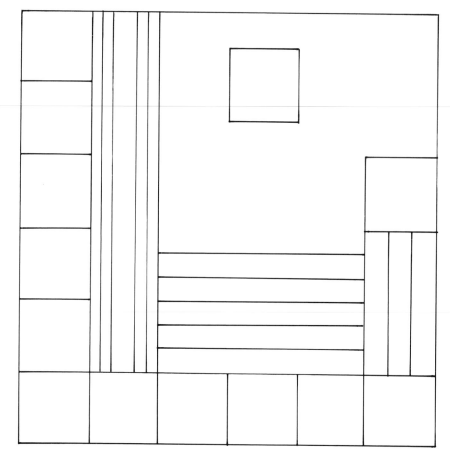

Fourth Coming

6-inch star block size
Size of quilt is 36-inches square

Poem is on page 13.

All of us remember our first big display of fireworks. I was so impressed with the beautiful bursts of color which seemed to hang in the sky ever so long. But the grand finale was an American flag which came alive with explosive red, white and blue, and glowed while our national anthem was played. Fireworks are still enjoyed, but none are as impressive as that beautiful flag.

I feel fortunate that our 200th celebration came within my lifetime, and that I got to see the whole nation celebrate with enthusiasm. One of the ways was the making of bicentennial quilts. Mine is a contemporary one. Even though the Bicentennial period has passed, it is never too late to record a memory of this eventful time.

Many different shades of reds, whites, and blues were used to give movement. The stars are of silk maurea taffeta and shimmer as if our nation's patriotism was shining through.

Fourth Coming quilt was pieced and quilted by Marty Caterino, East Lansing, Michigan. Marty does beautiful hand pieced quilts, but this was her very first machine pieced one. The workmanship is top grade. I hope this will encourage both beginning and experienced quilters to add this quilt to their collections.

First, you would piece the thirteen stars. Had you realized there were thirteen? All of the strips of fabric are 1-inch wide...sometimes two of the same color are together for a wider effect. The field of blue is broken down in many different pieces of the deeper blue fabric. The same breaking down of an area is reviewed under the quilt "Confusion" on page 62-63. When each area is diagonised, it really is quite simple to work out.

Fourth Coming quilt on page 11.

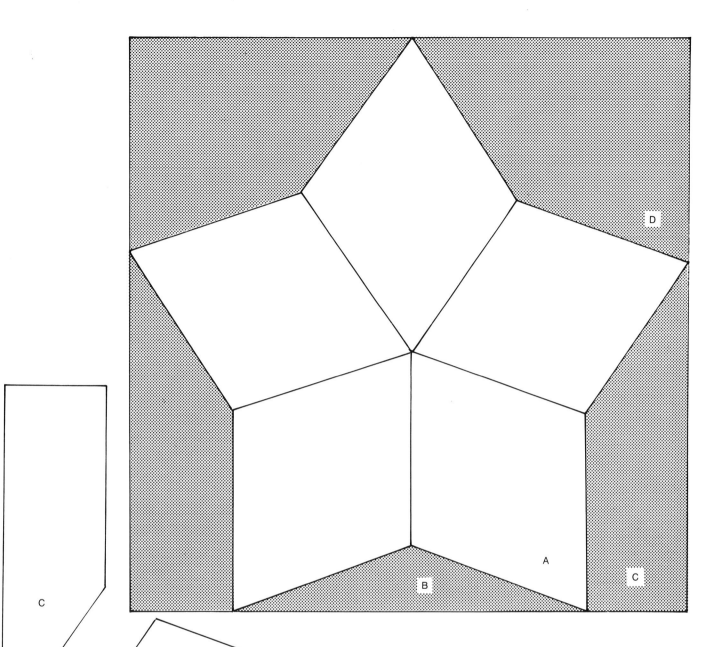

Five pointed star

6-inch block

This is not one of the easiest stars to draft out for a quilt. It is not that difficult to piece. Just a six inch size is given since that is one used for ''Fourth Coming'' quilt.

A – cut 5 star points, B – cut 1, C – cut 1 and 1 reversed, D – cut 1 and 1 reversed.

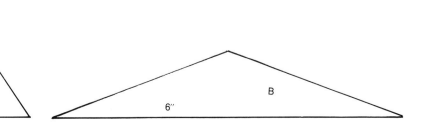

Confusion

Like most quilters, my mind is overflowing with ideas and plans for my next one hundred quilts. Those, coupled with family life and work life, occasionally add up to mass confusion. Hence, this quilt design. There are days when I'm sure if my brain was exposed, it would look exactly like this! Confusion quilt on back cover.

Confusion

Confusion

Amid daily confusion, there I sat
My forty-eleventh quilt upon my lap
Everyone hungry, even the cat
I stitch away and skip my nap
My fingers busy, my bottom fat
The baby is crying, give him a pat
Friends drop by for a friendly chat
Morning's mail on the front doormat
Need clean clothes, who said that
Mom, have you seen my ball and bat
Kids are fighting, tit for tat
House needs cleaning, imagine that!!

Size of quilt is 32-1/2 by 40-1/2-inches.
Border is 4-1/2-inches.

Confusion over which color to put where, confusion over solids versus prints, what size shall the finished piece be? Should it be a bed quilt or a quilt for the eye to enjoy on the wall?

A print fabric would be more effective for many of the traditional blocks. A print fabric also reminds one of a country decorating theme. But a solid color fabric can take the same country-looking piece and make it very contemporary in viewing. Bright, bold solids in high contrast placed in an interesting and angular way can achieve a wall quilt that will cause the viewer to take a second look.

If you are a traditional quilter, stretch your designing and quilting fun by following a very few simple guidelines. That is how this piece, ''Confusion,'' was created. ''Fourth Coming'' also uses these same ideas, but blends the row of five pointed stars down the side and across the bottom. See pages 60-61.

Take a piece of graph paper. Draw in your outside edge of the quilt. Then begin to break up various sections of the inside measurements by drawing straight and angular lines. Remember, avoid lines that go from one edge straight across to the other edge. Also, if you like an angular design, you will want to piece it. By keeping organized in this breakdown of the quilt, it will be easier to piece. For example, note in the sketch that there are areas that look like a simple four patch, a nine patch, areas of strips of fabric, etc.

In areas that look like a design hanging out in the middle, just connect them by a seam. As long as the two fabrics are the same color, the seams (once quilted) will not be visible to detract from the overall design. As a last resort, you may be required to applique a bit.

However, should you wish to use this as a guide for your first attempt at creating a contemporary wall quilt, be advised that this illustration is drawn over graph paper where 1/4-inch equals 1-inch (28 by 36-inches). Take a large sheet of graph paper and draw it out for your individual templates. You will find it more fun, less frustrating and more rewarding to just draw your very own design for a quilt.

A help in planning color placement is to use coloring pencils to color areas in to get the overall feeling of the quilt before going to fabric and stitching. Remember that fabric does give a different appearance than coloring, but you can get the general idea.

And most of all, enjoy experimenting. It could be your most memorable quilt yet.

Confusion quilt was pieced by Colleen Beach, Lansing, Michigan and quilted by Diana Outwin, Grand Haven, Michigan.

Last Piece II

My neighbor and I are making quilts of scraps
To warm our bones for a winter's nap.

Mine is a four-patch in beige and blue.
The colors so soft, pretty and new.

I'm missing a piece, it won't be right.
My friend may help me, yes she might.

Here she comes with the color I need.
I hug her and bless her for her good deed.

I sit here and relax in the shade of the tree
And admire my quilt and the help I received.

Where would I be without a friend to care,
a Fellow quilter, willing to share.

Antique Quilts and Blocks

Antique quilts found today are yesterday's memories which we have the good fortune to enjoy.

Antique quilts and blocks have not been neglected. Old quilts that have seen use have faded to beautiful soft hues, and are particularly pleasing to the eye. We have one, a neat variation of the Double Irish Chain, to share with you. Also, we have a beautiful, simple, old top, Brick Wall, which gives me pleasure just to look at it's colors of bright turkey red and white. Colors are still bright not having been exposed to the light and air of time in this top.

These old quilts are becoming more and more scarce and more expensive. However, there are ample antique blocks to be had at very reasonable prices. Many sets of these blocks have been broken up and sold separately, making it difficult to find enough to assemble large quilts. On the next few pages, you'll see how some of these old quilt blocks can be used. Most quilts are quite small, the largest measuring 48 by 64-inches, which is the perfect nap quilt.

In order for you to make modern day versions, patterns are given for each one.

But there is another way to search for old quilts or blocks. The next time you visit your Granny, Mother, favorite aunt or elderly family friend, ask if they just happen to have some old bits and pieces of patchwork blocks just laying around. You just might go home feeling like you struck gold with an old quilt top or at least a few blocks under your arm.

And think about the good feelings of the giver of these treasures. Someone actually wants those old blocks! Now they won't have to think about getting around to finishing them someday. Shared memories will flow as you are told about the fabrics, when they were put together, family ties that might not have been remembered for years.

You will remember these comments and a quilt history begins. Record them on the back of the piece for future generations to enjoy.

Several of these small quilts were grouped around what one might remember Grandma's house to be like. See page 14.

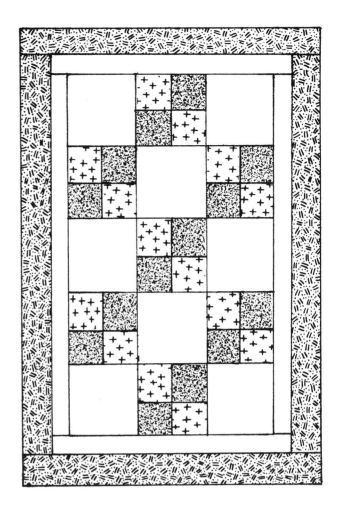

Four Patch Quilt

I made this quilt from old quilt blocks about five years ago, but never got around to binding it. In the meantime, the needed fabric was used for another project. When I decided to bind the quilt, alas, no matching fabric to be found.

So, the batting was trimmed and the front and back turned under 1/4-inch (into each other) and blind stitched closed. A line of quilting 1/2 inch in from the outside edge anchors the batting and also gives the effect of binding.

Many antique quilts were left unbound as this was a mundane task instead of a creative one. If you run against this problem, try this method of binding rather than by-pass a beautiful old quilt. By binding in this manner, you are not adding new fabric to the old therefore keeping the antique value.

Color photograph of this quilt on page 14.

Grape Basket Block

Grape Basket Quilt
4, 8 & 12 inch size block
4-inch would make quilt size 16
by 24-inches plus border.
8-inch would make quilt size 32
by 48-inches plus border.
12-inch would make quilt size 48
by 72-inches plus border.

The making of these blocks undoubtedly occupied some lady's idle hours, however, she was not a master quilter. Some pieces were cut on the bias, some parts had to be pieced in order to have enough fabric. Often times this was done in order to use every little bit of fabric. I fell in love with these blue and white blocks, flaws and all, but didn't want to make a quilt that required more work than the worth of the blocks. Hence, a tacked doll quilt.

Little people need quilts for their dolls, and one they've helped make will be more endearing than the professional quilt. The little girl in your life could arrange the blocks to please her eye, you could assemble and make the top ready for tacking. Tacking a quilt is a great first project for a child. The needle is of a size she can handle without becoming frustrated.

These quilts won't be of prize winning quality, but the child will treasure her own hand work, and she will have had a pleasant introduction to quilting. It will be her treasure.

The pattern is given in 4, 8 and 12-inch sizes for making quilts all the way from a doll bed size up to a bed size quilt.

Grape Basket quilt on page 14.

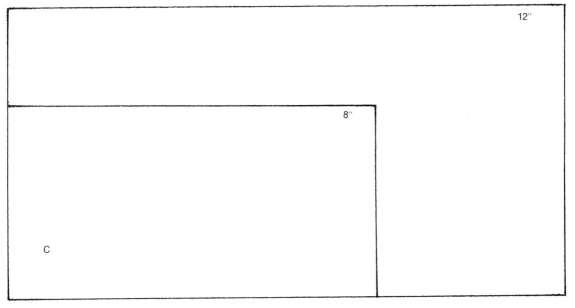

12"

8"

C

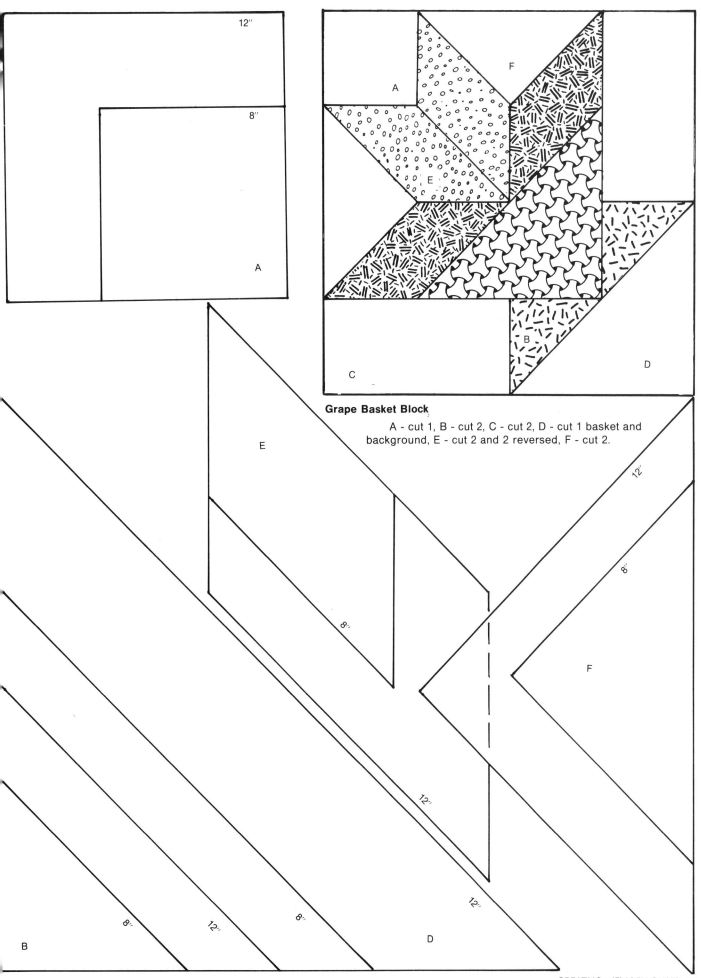

Grape Basket Block

A - cut 1, B - cut 2, C - cut 2, D - cut 1 basket and background, E - cut 2 and 2 reversed, F - cut 2.

Goose Tracks Quilt

Quilt size is 48 by 64-inches using 8-inch blocks.
Wall quilt size is 26 1/2-inch square using 8-inch blocks with 2-inch border

This quilt was made of antique blocks I'd had for sometime. While showing them to Betty Boyink and Milly Splitstone one night, ideas started to fly like sparks from a fire. We arranged them by distributing the colors in an eye pleasing manner and had one block left over. That block, added to the border, gives weight to the bottom. Three of the border fabrics were set into remaining corners.

When we decided on the placement of the blocks, we were working close up. It was not until the top was pieced and viewed from afar, that the effect of the white in the blocks was noticed. Viewed at a distance, the prints of the various fabrics and the actual block design were no longer what held the eye. The white pieces appeared to be birds in flight, giving these old quilt blocks a contemporary look. It was then that we decided on the quilting design; half circles for the blocks and slanting lines for the border. The four corner blocks were quilted following the pieced lines of the goose tracks block.

When setting together blocks for a new quilt top, make one (or four) corner block for your border using the same colors, but an entirely different block design. Blocks set side by side can lose their identity, one pulled out to the border makes the statement.

The small wall hanging set on point gives an entirely different look to the same block.

Many quilters have odd antique blocks that they just couldn't resist buying. Try our method of putting them to good use. Goose tracks pattern is on page 42 in Geese on Parade section.

Assembled by Betty Boyink, Grand Haven, Michigan, quilted by Connie Hartwick, Mason, Michigan.

The photograph of the quilt is on page 14.

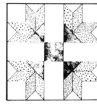

Irish Chain Variation

15-inch block size, 9-inch solid block
Quilt size is 84 by 84 inches
Border size is 3-inches.

Take a closer look at the artwork above. At first glance, it appears to be just an Irish Chain quilt. This one is in the quilt collection of Milly Splitstone of Fremont, Michigan. It is off-set just enough that a whole interesting new design emerges. The traditional Irish chain, at right, is easily assembled in blocks, but this quilter changed it enough that this was lost. A darker outline is around one block. One can imagine that quilter might have looked quickly at an Irish Chain, but couldn't quite remember how it went together so put hers together the way she remembered.

To piece this quilt, you will need to make a 3-inch square template. One block consists of 13 dark and 12 light squares. The solid blocks are a 9-inch square.

Irish Chain quilt on page 14.

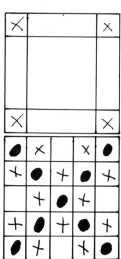

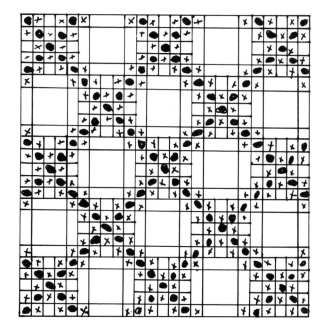

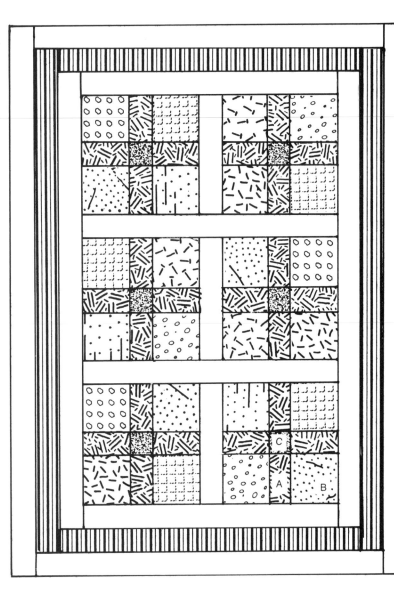

Save-All Quilt

Size of quilt is 30 by 40-inches using 8-inch blocks.

These six blocks were one of my finds. When deciding to set them together, I began to wonder why they had seemed attractive. The rust rectangles were the only color they had in common, making the blocks seemingly impossible to match with our modern day fabrics. To pick up just the rust made for a very dull quilt. To pick up any of the other colors made the rust in the blocks look a terrible mistake.

At this point, I decided the quilter who pieced these blocks many years ago had realized the same problem. So doing, she laid them aside and went on to bigger and better things. That thought only made me more determined they should not spend the next 100 years in the back of a drawer.

Maybe a stripe! A rust and gold stripe was finally chosen which helped pull the blocks together. Keep stripes in mind when working with difficult color combinations. Ones with a neutral background are particularly useful.

You may check out the success of this choice in the color photograph of the quilt on page 14.

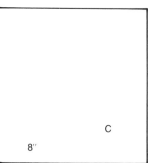

C

8″

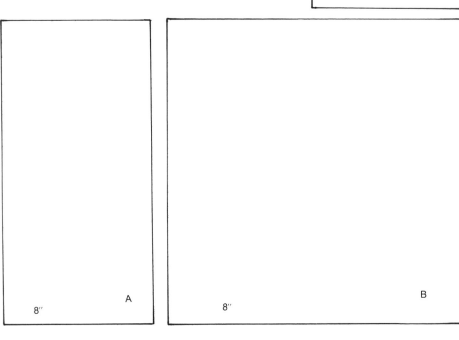

A

8″

B

8″

Nine Patch

To sit and quilt is no longer a chore,
It used to be work, but not anymore.

You can sit and quilt by the hour and plan,
All the patterns and designs to be sewn by hand.

Red hearts and flowers, green leaves and trees,
Or you can use other colors, if you please.

There's no end to all you can sew,
You can make small quilts or quilts that grow.

Mini quilts, wall quilts, make what you choose,
Mine's a nine patch in shades of blue.

Nine Patch

The nine patch is an early simple quilt block. It can be used side by side, separated by sashing, or the nine patch makes a very good corner block for a border. This was done on page 28 for the outer border of Madonna's Memory Sampler Quilt.

To make the size pattern required, simply divide the space equally into thirds.

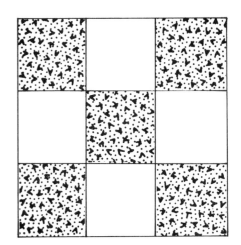

"Favorite Chore II"
© Madonna Ferguson 1985

Favorite Chore

When I was little, I had my own quilt,
I hugged it and dragged it around without guilt.

It was there when I was tired and when I was sad,
All the bright colors soon making me glad.

What fun to sit in the middle and choose,
Which pieces for dresses to match my new shoes.

I grew older and I grew taller,
Still there are times I wish I were smaller.

I work when I should and work when I oughta,
And now make quilts for my own young daughter.

Brick Wall Quilt

Brick pattern given below.
Size of quilt is 70 by 95-inches
Border is 5-inches wide.

This lovely old quilt top is owned by Milly Splitstone of Fremont, Michigan, and I lust after it. It is turkey red and white. This is a quilt design that is simple enough for a beginner, yet so striking as to "hook" experienced quilters. Blue and white would make this an eyecatching quilt also. Sometimes the Brick Wall is called Streak of Lightening.

The Brick Wall pattern would be a suitable gift for a man or boy in your life, or for those young students who would like a quilt in their school colors. Let's face it. Some school's colors are enough to make you want to throw up! Short of insisting they choose a school with colors pleasing to your eye, this would be a quick and easy way to help make those school years more memorable.

The quilt top is photographed in a hoop frame on a Grandma's porch on page 14.

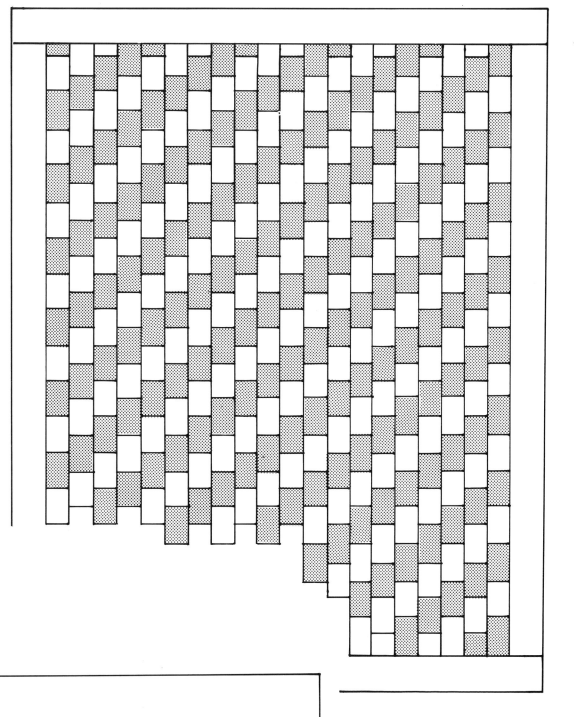

Showing Off

Mommy and Daddy went to the mill, the cows have to be fed,
You should see all those sacks of feed stacked in the shed.

My sister and I climbed all over the pile,
Visions of pretty dresses, but it would be yet a while.

When the sacks were emptied, washed, dried, and pressed,
Granny sewed, see how pretty we're dressed.

Morning Song

When you awaken each morning ready for play,
First kneel on your knees, fold your hands, and pray.

Now that your day has started out right,
Wonderful things are within your sight.

Fresh flowers in Mommy's garden to smell,
Sweet spring water from hidden wells.

A ride with Daddy over the fields,
Or finding blackberries deep in the hills.

Or maybe just a clear sweet song,
From a single blue bird as you stroll along.

All these things are yours to keep.
Remember them at night as you drift into sleep.

One of the things that makes the world go round,
Is the single bird's clear sweet sound.

"Going to the Fair" a Madonna Ferguson 1985

Going to the Fair

On our way to see Cinderella, we
     drove by the fair,
The bright lights, ferris wheel, and
     music made us long to be there.

Cinderella was quickly forgotten, our decision was made,
We had to go, the memories would never fade.

Our eyes were wide as we took in the sights,
Ate hotdogs and cotton candy down to the last bite.

We pitched pennies at bottles and rode the merry-go-round,
An hour later, the swings we found.

Our brother, Joe, bought us bright balloons filled with "funny air".
See mine away up there.

The Roman Stripe quilt with its many variations makes an
excellent quilt to use when drawing scenes. See page 53 for this
quilt technique.

Granny's Lesson

To embroidery, my Granny taught me how
This I do to while away the hours, then and now.

To work with my hands, I seem to have the knack
When I try real hard, you can't tell front from back.

Granny's ninety-four now, and her sight is poor
Oh, how I wish we were young once more
To sit at her knee and listen to lore.

How wonderful it is to have such a friend
And the knowledge that my Granny's love will never end.

Practice Makes Perfect

Practice makes perfect, or so they say.
I've been practicing the live long day.

My stitches seem better than they did before.
Mommy said, Lovely, but practice some more.

I checked my stitches and they looked good to me.
If I can't quit soon, I'll miss the doll's tea.

Mommy counted my stitches and said,
Is that what they taught in the books you've read?

Mommy, can I quit, it's almost noon.
She smiled and said, I could pretty soon.

I worked right along and Mommy seemed stearn
But she was right, a lesson I learned.

I checked again and my stitches were true
Practice makes perfect, see my quilt that's new.

'Practice Makes Perfect'
© Madonna Ferguson 1985

"Company's Coming"
© Madonna Ferguson 1985

Company's Coming

We've cleaned all morning and finished our chores,
Granny baked pies, Mommy did floors.

The ladies are coming to visit and have tea,
We'll have to sit as good as can be.

They'll talk about things we don't know,
The afternoon will pass so terribly slow.

Little girls should be seen and not heard they believe,
What, oh what, we have a reprieve?
We can greet them with flowers and then we can leave?

We'll go to the creek and then to the woods to play,
How long did you say the ladies will stay?

We must hurry, we must run really fast,
Before you know it, the day will be past!

Visiting

A pitch-in lunch and a quilting bee.
Work to do and friends to see.

We'll stitch and chat until noontime break.
Then relax, stretch and ease the ache.
How many quilts did we make?

The hostess smiles and does the count.
Nine quilts, such a large amount.

Back to work. The afternoon's chore?
Nine quilts? Even more!

Twenty tops were quilted this day.
A productive one, wouldn't you say?

Country Days Remembered

Growing up on a farm has to be one of the world's most wonderful gifts to children. Some portions of that gift were not truly appreciated until, as an adult, I moved to the city.

My memories of growing up in the country include the smell of fresh mowed hay, fields to roam, a pond to fish, creeks to swim in, shady woods for cool afternoon walks, apple trees with sweet spring blossoms and late summer fruit, new kittens in the barn, the excitement of the first garden plants peeking out of the soil, picking wild blackberries, making jams, jellies and pies, stringing green beans to dry (leather britches), canning season with jars of fruits and vegetables lining the cellar shelves, new dresses from feed sacks (I'm still a "clothes horse" and "fabricholic"), planting flowers each spring, my brothers studying by coal oil lamps (electricity was installed by the time my turn came around), making snow ice cream (fresh snow, bit of sugar, vanilla, and milk; mix quickly and eat before it melts - delicious), choosing and cutting cedar Christmas trees, picking wild flowers, riding the tractor with Daddy, curling up on Mommy's lap after all the others had left for school (Yes, I still call her Mommy).

Now, don't think I'm looking back through rose colored glasses. I also remember the chigger bites, bee stings, falling out of the barn loft, scratches from blackberry bushes, sunburns, mumps, measles, getting lost in the woods, and weeding tobacco beds for hours. However, you'll notice this list isn't as long as my "good memories" list.

Now that I have children of my own, live in a house with all the modern conveniences on a quiet residential street, *purchase* my canned goods, *buy* all of my clothes, I am amazed at all that my parents and grandparents accomplished. The first modern convenience we got on the farm was electricity, then running water. I think I was twelve when the inside bath was installed in place of a "path." Daddy was an electrician and worked a full time job besides working the farm. Of course, when they were old enough, my brothers worked it too. My Mommy and Granny raised the garden, canned, baked, cleaned, cooked, sewed, and helped with the farm. I seem to remember my sister and me playing more than working, but some of it must have rubbed off because we are both pretty good cooks and housekeepers *when we want to be.*

Maybe people growing up in a big city have just as many wonderful memories, but somehow, I doubt it.

I hope the stenciled scenes, poems, and quilts have given inspiration, sparked memories, and brought some joy to your lives. Thank you for taking this trip down memory lane with me. And I hope it has inspired you to travel your own memory lane . . . creating memory quilts to leave your own quilting legacy.

Also, I would like to take this opportunity to thank my parents and grandparents, my brothers and my sister for supplying my life with these memories and many more.

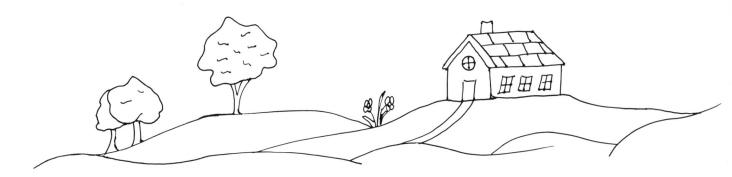

Bibliography

Beyer, Jinny, The Quilter's Album of Blocks & Borders
    EPM Publications, 1980

Brackman, Barbara, An Encyclopedia of Pieced Quilt Patterns
    Prairie Flower Publications, 1983

Hall, Carrie A. and Rose G. Kretsinger, Romance of Patchwork Quilt in America,
    The Caxton Printers, Ltd. 1935

Houck, Carter & Myron Miller, American Quilts and How to Make Them
    Charles Scribner's Sons, 1975

Hinson, Dolores A, A Quilter's Companion
    Arco Publishing Co., 1973

Khin, Yvonne M., The Collector's Dictionary of Quilt Names & Patterns
    Acropolis Books Ltd, 1980

Ickis, Marguerite, Standard Book of Quilt Making and Collecting
    Dover Publications, Inc., 1949

Malone, Maggie, 1001 Patchwork Designs
    Sterling Publishing Co., 1982

Rehmel, Judy, Key to 1000 Quilt Patterns
    Rehmel

The United States Patchwork Pattern Book from "Hearth & Home" Magazine